SIMPLE MALAY

TEXT OF LESSONS
ENGLISH TRANSLATIONS
BILINGUAL VOCABULARY
EXPLANATIONS OF GRAMMAR
MALAY-ENGLISH DICTIONARY
TRAVEL GUIDE TO MALAYSIA

Edited by
Tuminah Sapawi, B.A.

Europhone Language and Management Institute Pte Ltd
#04-33 Peninsula Shopping Centre, Coleman Street, Singapore 179804

Europhone Language & Management Institute Pte Ltd
#04-33 Peninsula Shopping Centre
3 Coleman Street
Singapore 179804

Europhone Language Institute
122 Campbell Shopping Complex
Jalan Dang Wangi, 50100
Kuala Lumpur
Malaysia

ISBN 981-3019-17-4

Acknowledgements

The picture on the cover of this book was made available by the courtesy of the **Great Wall Photographers Sdn. Bhd.**

Many of the pictures in the Travel Guide to Malaysia appear by the courtesy of **Iostech Marketing Sdn. Bhd.**

The map of Kuala Lumpur appears by the courtesy of the **Tourist Development Corporation (TDC), Malaysia.**

CONTENTS

YOUR TEACHERS

Miss Tuminah bte Sapawi
B.A., National University of Singapore
Native Speaker of Malay

Mr Mohammad Ishak
Certificate-in-Education
Teachers Training College, Singapore
Author and Teacher

Miss Sandra Hurst
B.A. (Hons), PGCE,
Warrick University, UK
Native Speaker of English

MALAYSIA AND ITS NEIGHBOURS

WELCOME TO MALAYSIA

Geographical Features
West Malaysia is about 750 miles long and 200 miles broad.
The isthmus of Kra that links it to Thailand is about 40 miles in width. The tip of the peninsula is joined to the island of Singapore by a short causeway across the Singapore Strait. On the east is the South China Sea and on the west, the Straits of Malacca. A discontinuous mountainous range runs from the north to the south. The highest point is Gunung Tahan (7,186 ft.). Separated by the South China Sea is East Malaysia's Sarawak and Sabah. Mt. Kinabalu, 13,455 ft. in Sabah, is popular with mountain climbers.

Climate
Malaysia enjoys tropical sunshine throughout the year. Rain falls intermittently during the changing of the monsoons, especially at the end of the year. Frequent brief showers cool the days when temperatures can vary from 21°C — 32°C. The average annual rainfall for West Malaysia is 100 inches. Lush equatorial vegetation covers the entire region. The mountainous slopes of Sabah and Sarawak receive up to 200 inches of rainfall.

The People
About half of the population of West Malaysia is Malay whereas in Sabah and Sarawak two-thirds of the population are indigenous. The Chinese comprise about 34% of the population of Malaysia while the Indians and Pakistanis make up 10%. The population of Malaysia is estimated at 16 million.

The Economy

The export of raw materials is one of the principal sources of revenue. Malaysia is among the world's leading exporters of tin, rubber and palm oil. Petroleum and gas found in the sea beds of the East Coast of the peninsula and in Sarawak have contributed significantly to the prosperity of the country. The manufacturing sector is active processing tin, rubber and palm oil. Other industries include lumbering, handicrafts, food and beverage production, metal forging and oil refining. More than 10% of the population is active in manufacturing.

Much land in West Malaysia, Sarawak and Sabah is still jungle with great potential for development. The cultivated plains yield rubber, palm oil, cocoa, coconut, rice, pineapple, tea and sugar cane. Jungle produce such as resin, rattan, gum and timber also contribute to the economic well being of the country. Sarawak exports pepper. Malaysia's major imports are machinery, manufactured goods, transport equipment, chemicals, medicine, food and live animals.

Formation of Malaysia

In 1963 Malaysia was formed as a constitutional monarchy within the Commonwealth of Nations with Tengku Abdul Rahman (1902 - 1990) as the first prime minister. He stayed in office till 1970. The present prime minister is Datuk Seri Dr Mahathir Mohamad. In 1966 the eleven states of the peninsula were re-named as West Malaysia. Kuala Lumpur is the capital. Its head of state, the Yang di-Pertuan Agong, or paramount ruler is chosen for a 5-year term from the 9 hereditary monarchs of the Malay States — Pahang, Perak, Johore, Kelantan, Trengganu, Kedah, Selangor, Negeri Sembilan and Perlis. Two other states, Malacca and Pulau Pinang (Penang) have no rulers. West Malaysia is 50,700 square miles in area.

East Malaysia

When West Malaysia came into existence, the former British colonies of North Borneo (now Sabah) and Sarawak became part of it as East Malaysia. Kota Kinabalu is the capital of the former and Kuching of the latter. The total area of the two territories is 128,338 square miles.

Government

Malaysia has a federal form of government. The prime minister wields executive power and is the leader of the majority party or coalition in the house of representatives. He is appointed by the head of state and the cabinet. He and his cabinet ministers are responsible to parliament which meets in Kuala Lumpur. It comprises a lower house of representatives and a senate. Representatives are elected for 5-year terms. Senators serve for 6 years.

Research Unit
Europhone Institute

HOW TO USE THIS COURSE

Aims

This course has been developed to enable you to acquire a basic knowledge of Malay in a short time. It is designed to give you a good foundation through study materials and the use of everyday, practical conversations.

Course Make-Up

The text is divided into ten selected lessons each of which has three sections. Part One is a dialogue in modern spoken Malay. A translation of it is given in English. Part Two is an Malay-English vocabulary list. Part Three comprises notes on Malay grammar. In these sections you have all the essentials to learn Malay. To help you master spoken Malay all the lessons have been recorded in audio-cassettes.

Method

First listen to Lesson 1 on the cassette. Let the teacher read. Follow the written sentences in the book. Stop the cassette at the end of each lesson. Rewind and play the cassette again from the beginning. Speak after the teacher, phrase by phrase or sentence by sentence in the pauses provided. Do this several times with each paragraph until you are satisfied with your pronunciation as compared with the model voices. Then move on to a new paragraph. Proceed in this manner.

Next study the Vocabulary, Translations and Explanations of each Lesson. Read, think and learn the Malay words and their meanings. Words are for your speech and the understanding of other people. Learn as many words as you can. Understand the rules of grammar so that you can make your own sentences. Study a little everyday. Don't forget to revise.

Practise speaking Malay in the beginning with your cassettes later with people. Make this a habit. Your success with Malay is assured.

Pronunciation

Should you have this book without cassettes, read the page on *Pronunciation* for your guidance.

Counter Readings for Cassette(s)

For easy winding of the cassette to the Lesson you wish to study, the cassette player's Counter Readings are given.

Counter Readings for Cassette(s)

Lessons	1	2	3	4	5	6	7	8	9	10
Single Cassette	*Side A* 0	43	99	167	247	*Side B* 0	61	116	188	288
Cassette No 1 Two Cassettes	*Side A* 0	64	*Side B* 0	82	*Cassette Side A* 0	*No 2* 78	*Side B* 164	0	71	169

Academic Advisory Board

PRONUNCIATION

The following explanations provide a guide to pronunciation for learners without the cassettes of this course.

Vowels

A vowel is a speech sound produced without an audible stopping of the breath and is expressed by certain letters of the alphabet:

Examples of Vowels	Malay Words	English Meanings
a as in mask As the last letter of a Malay word it is soft as in China.	masok saya	enter I, me
e as in red	lewat	late
i as in finish	kini	now
o as in boat	botol	bottle
u as in too!	tentu	certain

Diphthongs

Malay has only two diphthongs, a union of two vowel letters or sounds.

Examples of Diphthongs	Malay Words	English Meanings
ai as in aisle	balai	station, kiosk
au as in **ow** of **now**	halau	drive away (persons)

Consonants

A consonant is a speech sound produced by a full or partial stoppage of the breath and is expressed by certain letters of the alphabet.

Examples of Consonants	Malay Words	English Meanings
b as in English but as **p** when it is the last letter of a word	**b**alik	return
c as in **c**hurch	**c**abut	flee
d as in English **t** when it is the last letter of a word.	a**d**a	have
dz as in **th** of **that**:	Ram**dz**an	name of the fasting month
f (Arabic sound), it is often substituted by **p**	**f**asal (or **p**asal)	reason
g as in **g**oing	**go**sok	polish
h as in English, with 4 variations: (i) as the first letter of a word, it may be silent	**h**ujan	rain

	(ii) between 2 identical vowels it is distinctly pronounced	Pahang	name of a state in Malaysia
	(iii) between 2 different vowels, it is silent	pahit (or pait)	bitter (of taste)
	(iv) as the last letter of a word, it must be pronounced	sala**h**	incorrect, wrong
j	as in **j**udge	**j**atuh	fall
k	as in English	**k**asut	shoe
kh	(Arabic sound), it is frequently substituted by **k**	**kh**ayal	fantasy
l	as in English	bata**l**	cancel
m	as in English	**m**asak	cook
n	as in English	**n**aik	climb
ny	as in **ni** of onion	**ny**ior	coconut
ng	as in **ng**, of ding-dong	ba**ng**un	stand
p	as in English	**p**angkat	rank
r	as in **r**oar	**r**ampas	seize
s	as in **s**weet, (softly)	**s**enyum	smile
sh	as in English	**sh**ak	suspicion
t	as in English	**t**ikus	mouse
w	as in English	**w**akil	representative
y	as in **y**et	**y**atim	orphan
z	as in English	**z**ina	adultery

MALAY MISUSED

The following Malay words are often misused. In some cases they should not be used at all.

1 **banyak** = many, much   (correct)
  banyak buku = many books   (correct)
  banyak kerusi = many chairs   (correct)

Do not use the expression, **banyak baik** as it is incorrect. If paying a compliment then say:
    baik sekali   )
    baik sungguh) = very good
    baik sangat   )

2 **buat** = do, perform
  buat apa? = what are (you) doing?
  buat kerja = (I) am working.
The pronouns (often not spoken) are understood.
Do not use **bikin** as a synonym for **buat.** It is better not to use the word at all.

3 **beri** or **berikan** = to give.
Beri dia buku itu. Give him that book.
Bagi may be used as a less formal substitute. Do **not** use **kasi** as a synonym. It is Bazaar Malay and is best not used.

4 **punya** = a word used in Bazaar Malay to express possession,
  e.g. (a) **dia punya buku** = his book (incorrect)
     (b) **saya punya buku** = my book (incorrect)

Do not use **punya** at all.

Instead omit it and re-arrange the remaining words in the examples (a) and (b) and you get:
    buku dia = his book (correct)
    buku saya = my book (correct)

USERS OF OUR COURSES

SOME UNIVERSITIES, COLLEGES, SCHOOLS AND ORGANISATIONS WORLDWIDE WHICH USE EUROPHONE LANGUAGE COURSES

UNIVERSITIES
Srinakhrinwiron University, Thailand
University of Oregon, USA
University of Medison, Wisconsin, USA
University of Malaya
University of Technology
University Sains Malaysia, Penang
University of Singapore
University of Brunei, Darussalam

HIGH SCHOOLS
Kong Yiong High School
Presbyterian High School
Hai Sing Girls High School
St Theresa's High School
Chung Hwa High School
Tuan Mong High School
Anglican High School

SECONDARY SCHOOLS
Willow Avenue Secondary School
Westlake Secondary School
Woodlands Secondary School
Naval Base Secondary School
Boon Lay Secondary School
Yuan Ching Secondary School
Manjusri Secondary School
Tanjong Katong Girls' School
Victoria School
Yuying Secondary School
New Town Secondary School
Whampoa Secondary School
Telok Kurau Secondary School
Sekolah Menengah Alirshad, Pow
Sekolah Menengah Sultanah
Shuqun Secondary School

INTERNATIONAL ORGANISATIONS
New Zealand High Commission, Singapore
UNESCO, Bangkok
Telecoms, Singapore
Foreign Language Pte Ltd, Melbourne
Intertaal, Amsterdam
Asian Inst of Technology, Bangkok
POSB, Singapore
Ministry of Defence, Singapore
Petronas, Malaysia
Arab-Malaysian Development Bank
Arkib Negara, Malaysia
Sime Darby Planatations Bhd
Dunlop Malaysian Industry
Shell Malaysia Sdn Bhd
Canadian High Commission (KL)
American Embassy, Thailand

COLLEGES AND INSTITUTES
Institute Piawian Dan Penyelidikan
Forest Research Institute
Institute Penyelidikan dan Pertanian
Institute Technology Mara
Maktab Kerjasama Malaysia
SEAMO Regional Centre, Penang
Institute Perdagangan Mara
Ngee Ann Polytechnic
Institute Kemahiran Mara, PJ (MARA)
Vocational & Industrial Training Board

PRIMARY SCHOOLS
Yuqun Primary School
Jin Tai Primary School
Qifa Primary School
Poi Ching Primary School
Beatty Primary School
Fuchun Primary School
Nan Hua Primary School
Beng Wan Primary School
Haig Boys' Primary School

xvi

Perempuan Muda	**Selamat pagi.**
	Good morning.
Lelaki Muda	**Selamat pagi.**
	Good morning.
Perempuan Muda	**Apa khabar anda hari ini?**
	How are you today?
Lelaki Muda	**Agak baik, terima kasih. Dan anda?**
	Quite well, thank you. And you?
Perempuan Muda	**Saya sakit kepala.**
	I have a headache.

1

Lelaki Muda	**Saya dukacita mendengar itu.** I'm sorry to hear that.
Perempuan Muda	**Sakitnya tidak berat.** It's not serious.
Lelaki Muda	**Anda perlu berjumpa doktor.** You should see a doctor.
Perempuan Muda	**Saya akan berjumpanya hari ini.** I'll be seeing him today.
Lelaki Muda	**Anda hendak ke rumah sakitkah?** Are you going to the hospital?
Perempuan Muda	**Tidak, saya akan berjumpa doktor keluarga.** No, I'm going to the family doctor.
Lelaki Muda	**Di manakah keliniknya?** Where is his clinic?
Perempuan Muda	**Ianya di jalan berhampiran.** It's in a nearby street.
Lelaki Muda	**Saya akan ke pejabat saya.** I'm going to my office.
Perempuan Muda	**Anda terlalu awal.** You're very early.
Lelaki Muda	**Ya, benar.** Yes, it's true.
Perempuan Muda	**Saya tak mahu melewatkan anda.** I won't delay you.
Lelaki Muda	**Tak mengapa.** That's all right.

Perempuan Muda	**Selamat jalan.**
	Have a good day.
Lelaki Muda	**Selamat tinggal.**
	Good-bye.

Perbendaharaan Kata **Vocabulary** **Part 2**

selamat pagi	a form of greeting; good morning
apa	how; in what way
khabar	news
awak	you
hari ini	today
agak baik	quite well
terima kasih	an expression of gratitude
dan	and
saya	I
ucap selamat	greetings
perempuan muda	young girl
lelaki muda	young man
sakit kepala	pain in the head, headache
dukacita	feeling regret
mendengar	to hear
itu	that
berat	serious; heavy
perlu	must; ought to
berjumpa	to visit; to consult
doktor	doctor; physician

1

rumah sakit	hospital
kelinik	clinic
keluarga	family; parents and children
berhampiran	nearby; not far from
jalan	a road
pejabat	office
terlalu	very
awal	early; before an appointed time
ya	answer to something in the affirmative
tak akan	will not; having no intention to
melewatkan	to delay
tak mengapa	don't worry; that's all right
selamat jalan	a greeting to someone going off
selamat tinggal	a greeting to someone staying behind
kepala	head
sakit	pain
akan	will
di mana	where
di	at, in
mana	where
benar	true
ya	yes
mahu	want, desire
tidak (tak)	not; not
anda	you (polite form)
ke	to
rumah sakit	hospital
kah	a suffix expressing a question

Penerangan   **Explanations   Part 3**

1. **Kependekan (Abbreviations)**

    In conversation, we sometimes shorten words, eg.

tak = tidak	no
tak mahu	don't want
tak ada	not having
tak mengapa	that's all right
nak = hendak	want; desiring something
nak/hendak makan	want to eat
nak/hendak pergi	want to go

    There are many such examples.

2. **Ucapan-ucapan** (greetings)

    Common greetings are:

Selamat pagi	good morning
Selamat petang	good afternoon
Selamat malam	good night
Selamat datang	welcome
Selamat berjumpa	nice to see you
Selamat berkenalan	nice to know you;

3. **Sakitnya.** This word combines the noun *sakit* (pain) with the pronoun *nya* (it), for the full meaning, *its pain*.

4. **....tidak berat.** These words mean *not serious.* **Tidak** (no, not) is used to express the negative, eg.

(i) Tidak, mahu.

(I) do not want (it).

Malay being a precise language omits words which are understood. Hence, the pronouns *I* and *it* are not expressed in the above Malay sentence.

5. **Nouns**

As with English, Malay nouns are words or phrases used as names of persons, places or things, eg.

Malay	English	Remarks
Enche Ali	− Mr Ali	A common name
Kuala Lumpur	− Kuala Lumpur	The capital of Malaysia
rumah	− a house	
buku	− a book	

6. **Plural of Nouns**

The way to express the plural of a noun is to repeat the noun word with a hypen between the two words. eg

Singular Nouns	Plural Nouns
kedai = shop	**kedai-kedai** = shops
pensel = pencil	**pensel-pensel** = pencils

Repetition is unnecessary *if* an adjective expressing quantity precedes the noun. eg

buku = book	**banyak buku** = many books
budak = child	**ramai budak** = many children

PELAJARAN 2   LESSON 2   Part 1

BERJUMPA SEORANG KAWAN   MEETING A FRIEND

Perempuan Muda	**Siapa itu?**
	Who is it?
Lelaki Muda	**Saya.**
	It's me.
Perempuan Muda	**Selamat berjumpa kembali.**
	It's nice to see you again.
Lelaki Muda	**Baikkah anda?**
	Are you better?
Perempuan Muda	**Baik sedikit. Dan bagaimana anda?**
	Much better. And how are you?

Lelaki Muda	**Penat sedikit. Saya baru datang dari pejabat.**
	A little tired. I've just come from the office.
Perempuan Muda	**Sila duduk. Di mana pejabat anda?**
	Do sit down. Where is your office?
Lelaki Muda	**Ianya di dalam bandar.**
	It is in the city.
Perempuan Muda	**Bagaimana anda pergi ke pejabat?**
	How do you go to your office?
Lelaki Muda	**Saya memandu ke sana.**
	I drive to it.
Perempuan Muda	**Pukul berapa pejabat anda di buka?**
	What time does your office open?
Lelaki Muda	**Ia di buka pada pukul 9 pagi.**
	It opens at 9 a.m.
Perempuan Muda	**Pukul berapa ianya ditutup?**
	What time does it close?
Lelaki Muda	**Ianya di tutup pada pukul 5 petang.**
	It closes at 5 p.m.
Perempuan Muda	**Bila anda makan tengah hari?**
	When do you have lunch?
Lelaki Muda	**Saya makan antara pukul 1 dan 2 petang.**
	I have it between 1 p.m. and 2 p.m.

Perempuan Muda	**Adakah anda bekerja pada hari-hari Sabtu?**
	Do you work on Saturdays?
Lelaki Muda	**Ya, saya bekerja.**
	Yes, I do.
Perempuan Muda	**Adakah anda bekerja sepanjang hari?**
	Do you work a full day?
Lelaki Muda	**Tidak.**
	No, I don't.

Perbendaharaan Kata   Vocabulary   Part 2

siapa	a pronoun (who) uséd only for persons
kembali	once more
baik sedikit	a little better
di mana	where
pejabat	office
bandar	large and important town
pergi	go
memandu	drive; to control a vehicle
pukul	time
makan tengah hari	meal taken in the middle of the day, lunch
antara	between; in the middle of two things
petang	afternoon
Sabtu	Saturday
sepanjang	full
hari	day; time between sunrise and sunset

penat	tired
datang	arrive
baru	just, new
dari	from
sila	please
duduk	sit
ia	it
ianya	its
ke	to (direction)
sana	there
berapa	how many
buka	open
tutup	close
bila	when
dan	and
bekerja	work
pada	at, in
hari-hari	every; daily
kah	suffix used to indicate a question eg. **adakah anda pergi?**
pergi	go

Penerangan   **Explanations**   **Part 3**

1. **Membuat perbandingan** (making comparisons)

   baik sedikit = a little better or better.

   baik sedikit has the same meaning as **lebih baik**.

   The three degrees of comparison are:

baik (good)

lebih baik (better)

sangat baik/terbaik (best)

In the superlative, the root word is usually preceded by **sangat** or **ter-**

Examples

Buku ini baik.	This is a *good* book.
Buku ini lebih baik.	This is a *better* book.
Buku ini sangat baik/terbaik.	This is the *best* book.

2. **Verbs**

A word whose functions is prediction, it performs in the same way in Malay, eg.

Buku itu jatuh.	The book *fell*.
Dia makan.	He *eats*.
Dia tangkap pencuri itu.	He *caught* the thief.

3. **Sepanjang** (from **panjang-** long) has more than one meaning. Idiomatic phrases include:

sepanjang hari	the whole day;
sepanjang jalan	all along the road
sepanjang pengetahuan saya	the period within my knowledge

PELAJARAN 3   LESSON 3   Part 1

KELUARGA SAYA   MY FAMILY

Lelaki Muda	**Adakah ini gambar keluarga anda?**
	Is this a picture of your family?
Perempuan Muda	**Ya, kami berempat, iaitu, ibu, bapa, abang dan saya.**
	Yes, there are four of us, my parents, my brother and I.
Lelaki Muda	**Di manakah bapa anda sekarang?**
	Where is your father now?
Perempuan Muda	**Ia sedang bekerja di ladangnya.**
	He is working on his farm.
Lelaki Muda	**Di manakah ibu anda?**
	Where is your mother?

Perempuan Muda	**Ia bersama-samanya di ladang.**
	She's with him on the farm.
Lelaki Muda	**Berapa umur abang anda?**
	How old is your brother?
Perempuan Muda	**Umurnya dua puluh tahun.**
	He is twenty years old.
Lelaki Muda	**Di mana ia bekerja?**
	Where does he work?
Perempuan Muda	**Ia bekerja di bandar.**
	He works in the city.
Lelaki Muda	**Adakah ini datuk anda?**
	Is this your grandfather?
Perempuan Muda	**Ya.**
	Yes.
Lelaki Muda	**Di mana datuk anda tinggal?**
	Where does your grandfather live?
Perempuan Muda	**Ia tinggal di kampung.**
	He lives in the countryside.
Lelaki Muda	**Ada kah ia tinggal seorang diri?**
	Does he live alone?
Perempuan Muda	**Tidak. Datuk saya tinggal bersama nenek saya.**
	No, my grandfather lives with my grandmother.
Lelaki Muda	**Berapakah umurnya?**
	How old is she?

3

Perempuan Muda	**Umurnya tujuh puluh tahun.**
	She's seventy years old.
Lelaki Muda	**Adakah anda mempunyai emak saudara?**
	Do you have an aunt?
Perempuan Muda	**Tidak, tetapi saya mempunyai seorang bapa saudara.**
	No, but I have an uncle.
	Saya juga ada dua orang sepupu.
	I also have two cousins.

Perbendaharaan Kata   Vocabulary   Part 2

gambar	picture
keluarga	family
ibu dan bapa	parents
abang	older brother
ibu/ emak	mother
umur	age
datuk	grandfather
nenek	grandmother
ibu/emak saudara	aunty
bapa saudara	uncle
sepupu	cousin (male or female)
anak saudara	nephew or niece
kami	we (including speaker)
berempat	the four (of us)

iaitu	that is
− kah	suffix indicating a question; a stress word
sekarang	now
sedang	word expressing continuous action
sedang bekerja	working
bekerja	work
ladang	farm
bersama	with
−nya	with him/her/it
tinggal	live
kampung	countryside, village
seorang	alone; one person
diri	self
umurnya	his/her age
umur	age
mempunyai	own, have
juga	also
ada	have, has
tetapi	but

Penerangan   Explanations   Part 3

1. **Abang** means elder brother and **Kakak**, elder sister;
    younger brother or sister is expressed by **adik**. e.g. **adik
    perempuan** is younger sister, and **adik lelaki**, younger
    brother.

    Bapa means father; another word popularly used is **ayah**.

2. **Adjective.** In English it is a word that describes a noun
    more fully. In Malay too, it performs the same function
    and is characterised by being placed **after** the Malay noun, eg.

Noun	Adjective	
buku	*merah*	*red* book
rumah	*baru*	*new* house
orang	*tua*	*old* man

3. **Keluarga anda. Anda** means *you* or *your* and is a polite form of address. When it is used after a noun (keluarga), it functions as an adjective. Hence in the above example, it means *your family.*

   keluarga anda = your family.

4. **Nouns with Prefixes**

Some **verbs** take one of two prefixes, either **pe** or **ke** to become **nouns**. The **pe** prefix may undergo euphonic changes. eg **peny, per**. It is by observing the use of such words that you will know which prefix to use as there are no definite rules. Part of the meaning of the root verb remains but a change in the meaning of the new word results.

Verbs	Nouns
pukul = hit, beat	**pemukul** = hammer
nyanyi = sing	**penyanyi** = singer
puji = to praise	**kepujian** = praise

5. **Conversion of Adjectives to Nouns**

Some adjectives lend themselves to change and become nouns by taking affixes. You should note such variations and add them to your knowledge since not all adjectives can be so converted, eg

Adjectives	Nouns
pandai = clever	**ke-pandai-an** = skill,
pakai = use	**pakaian** = clothes
sempit = narrow	**kesempitan** = narrowness.
perlu = useful	**keperluan** = requirement

PELAJARAN 4

BADAN

LESSON 4   Part 1

THE BODY

Saya mempunyai badan yang sihat.

I have a healthy body.

Saya bergerak ke sana sini dengan kaki.

I move about on my legs.

Saya gunakan tangan untuk mengangkat benda-benda.

I use my hands to carry things.

Saya ada sepasang tangan: kanan dan kiri.

I have a pair of hands: right and left.

Setiap tangan ada lima jari.

Each hand has five fingers.

Atas tengkuk saya ialah kepala saya.

Above my neck is my head.

4

Ada rambut atas kepala saya.

There is hair on my head.

Saya melihat dengan mata saya.

I see with my eyes.

Saya makan dengan mulut.

I eat with my mouth.

Dalam mulut ada gigi dan lidah.

There are teeth and a tongue in my mouth.

Saya gunakan telinga untuk mendengar.

I use my ears for hearing.

Saya bernafas melalui lubang hidung.

I breathe through my nostrils.

Saya mencium bau dengan hidung.

I smell with my nose.

Gigi digunakan untuk mengunyah makanan.

Teeth are used for chewing food.

Saya merasa makanan dan minuman dengan lidah.

I taste food and drinks with my tongue.

Bawah tengkuk dan leher saya ialah dada.

Below my neck is my chest.

Bawah dada saya ialah perut.

Below my chest is my stomach.

Saya duduk atas punggung saya.

I sit on my buttocks.

Perbendaharaan Kata   Vocabulary   Part 2

kepala   head

18

rambut	hair
muka	face
mata	eye or eyes
hidung	nose
lubang hidung	nostrils
mulut	mouth
gigi	tooth or teeth
lidah	tongue
telinga	ear or ears
leher	neck (front)
tengkuk	nape of neck
bahu	shoulder(s)
dada	chest
perut	stomach
pusat	navel
pinggang	hips
punggung	buttocks
lengan	arm
tangan	hand
pergelangan tangan	wrist
tapak tangan	palm of hand
jari (tangan)	fingers
kaki	leg
paha	thigh
lutut	knee
kepala lutut	knee-cap
buku lali	ankle

4

tapak kaki	sole of foot
jari kaki	toes
kuku	nail (of fingers or toes)
mengangkat	carry
benda	things
sepasang	a pair
kanan	right
kiri	left
atas	on top (of)
ialah	is
melihat	see
makan	eat
dalam	in
ada	there is/are
bernafas	breathe
melalui	through
mencium	smell
bau	odour
digunakan	is used (passive voice)
gunakan	use (active voice)
merasa	taste
makanan	food
bawah	under
duduk	sit
sihat	healthy
bergerak	move
ke sana	there

ke sini	here
dengan	with (preposition)
gunakan	use
untuk	for
mempunyai	own, possess (verb)
yang	which, who, that
setiap	each

Penerangan   Explanations   Part 3

1. **Badan** or **tubuh** means the *human body.*

    Badan can also mean *organization.*

    Kepala means *head.*

    Kepala is also used to mean *the head* or *chief* of an organization.

    Pusat besides meaning the *navel*, is also used for *centre*, e.g.

    pusat membeli belah shopping centre

    pusat perdagangan trading centre

    It is common to confuse between **bau** (smell) and **bahu** (shoulders). Another common word for *smell* or *sniff* is **cium**. The confusion arises because the **h** in **bahu** is silent.

    Mata and **telinga,** for example mean *the eye* and *ear* respectively, (for singular and plural). Emphasis of *both eyes* or *ears* is brought about by using the phrase **kedua-dua belah.** Further examples are:

    kedua-dua belah tangan = both hands

    kedua-dua belah kaki = both legs

4

2. The usual way of expressing the plural form in Malay is simply by repeating the word, e.g.

jari	=	finger
rumah	=	house
badan	=	body or organization
jari-jari	=	fingers
rumah-rumah	=	houses
badan-badan	=	bodies or organizations

Gigi, **rambut** and **kuku** are more often than not the plural; emphasis of the singular form is brought about by the use of a classifier, e.g. sebatang, sehelai.

sebatang gigi = a tooth

sehelai rambut = a strand of hair

There is no variation of **kuku** to express the plural. A classifier is also referred to as a numeral co-efficient.

3. **Pronouns**

Common Malay pronouns are:

dia	he, she, it
saya	I
anda (polite)	you
awak (to a subordinate)	you
engkau (-do-)	you (to stress superiority of speaker)
kita	we, our, us (includes speaker and others)

kami	we(excludes the listener)
kamu	you, your (excludes the speaker)
mereka	they, them

4. Duplication of Words

We learnt earlier that the plural of a noun may be expressed by the repetition of the noun. This repetitive device is also used for other purposes:

a **Expressing indefiniteness**

The idea is noticeable in the names of insects and creatures.

kelip-kelip	= fireflies
kupu-kupu	= butterflies
angkut-angkut	= mason bees
kura-kura	= tortoises

angkut = lift; berkelip-kelip = twinkling (of stars)

b **Indefinite plurality**

It is evident in indefinite pronouns, conjunctions and adverbs.

siapa-siapa (or sesiapa)	= anybody, whoever
mana-mana	= whichever, anywhere
beransur-ansur	= by instalments

siapa = who; mana = where

c **Continuity and intensity**

Please note the following examples:

menjerit-jerit	= shriek incessantly
berlari-lari	= run hurriedly
tiap-tiap	= each, every

jerit = shriek; lari = run

PELAJARAN 5   LESSON 5   Part 1

MASA   TIME

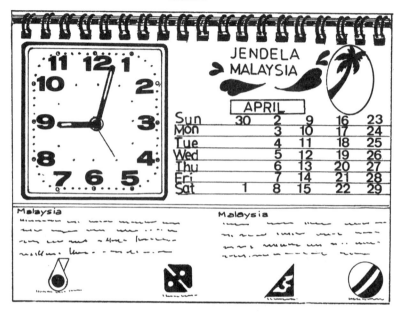

Ada dua puluh empat jam dalam sehari.

There are twenty four hours in a day.

Enam puluh minit menjadi satu jam.

Sixty minutes make an hour.

Enam puluh saat menjadi satu minit.

Sixty seconds make a minute.

Tujuh hari menjadi seminggu.

Seven days make a week.

Ada empat minggu dalam sebulan.

There are four weeks in a month.

Ada lima puluh dua minggu dalam setahun.

There are fifty-two weeks in a year.

Satu tahun ada tiga ratus enam puluh lima hari.

A year has three hundred and sixty-five days.

Satu bulan ada tiga puluh hari.

A month has thirty days.

Satu minggu ada tujuh hari.

A week has seven days.

Pukul dua belas siang disebut tengah hari.

12 noon is called midday.

Pukul dua belas malam disebut tengah malam.

12 o'clock at night is called midnight.

Matahari terbit pada pagi hari.

The sun rises in the morning.

Matahari terbenam pada petang hari.

The sun sets in the evening.

Makanan pada pagi hari disebut sarapan.

Food served in the morning is called breakfast.

Makanan pada tengah hari disebut makan tengah hari.

Makanan pada waktu malam disebut makan malam.

Food served at midday is called lunch. Food served at night is called dinner.

Hari-hari dalam seminggu ialah:	**Isnin, Selasa, Rabu, Khamis, Jumaat, Sabtu, Ahad atau Minggu.**
The days of the week are:	Monday, Tuesday, Wednesday, Thursday, Friday, Saturday and Sunday.

5

Perbendaharaan Kata   Vocabulary   Part 2

dua	two
dua puluh	twenty
empat	four
jam	hour
dalam	in
hari	day
sehari	a day
enam	six
enam puluh	sixty
minit	minutes
satu	one
jadikan; menjadi	make
minggu	week
seminggu	a week
sebulan	a month
lima	five
lima puluh	fifty
setahun	a year
dua belas	twelve
siang	daylight
hari	day
tengah hari	noon; midday
malam	night
tengah malam	midnight
matahari	sun

terbit	rises; appears (of the sun)
pagi	morning
terbenam	sets (of the sun)
petang	afternoon; evening
makanan	food
sarapan	breakfast
waktu	time
makan malam	dinner
disebut	is referred to; is mentioned
pada	at (used with time)

Penerangan   Explanations   Part 3

1. The prefix **se** is actually an abbreviation of **satu** meaning *one*, *a* or *an* ; e.g.

   sehari   a day

   sejam   an hour

2. **Ada dua puluh...** The verb **ada** means *there is* or *there are*.

3. Note that Malay is a precise language. Unnescessary words, and often pronouns are omitted in a sentence, e.g.
   Sudah makan?
   Have (you) eaten?
   The pronoun **you** has been omitted.

4. **Pukul berapa?** (What's the time?) is the commonest way of asking the time.

PELAJARAN 6	LESSON 6 Part 1
MENGIRA	**COUNTING**

Kita mesti tahu mengira.

We must know how to count.

satu	one
dua	two
tiga	three
empat	four
lima	five
enam	six
tujuh	seven
lapan	eight
sembilan	nine

sepuluh	ten
sebelas	eleven
dua belas	twelve
tiga belas	thirteen
empat belas	fourteen
lima belas	fifteen
enam belas	sixteen
tujuh belas	seventeen
lapan belas	eighteen
sembilan belas	nineteen
dua puluh	twenty

Sebut dua puluh satu hingga dua puluh sembilan; selepas itu tiga puluh.

Say twenty one till twenty nine; after that thirty.

Tiga puluh satu,   tiga puluh dua...   tiga puluh sembilan.

Thirty one,   thirty two ...   thirty nine.

Kemudian empat puluh.

Then forty.

Empat puluh campur sepuluh jadi lima puluh.

Forty increased by ten is fifty.

Jika kita teruskan campur sepuluh kita dapat:

If we continue adding ten, we get:

enam puluh	sixty
tujuh puluh	seventy
lapan puluh	eighty
sembilan puluh	ninety
seratus	one hundred

6

Seratus campur seratus jadi dua ratus; seterusnya sampai sembilan ratus.

One hundred increased by one hundred is two hundred; and so on till nine hundred.

Sepuluh ratus ialah seribu.

Ten hundreds make a thousand.

Seterusnya kita dapati:

As we proceed we get:

Sepuluh ribu hingga sembilan puluh sembilan ribu. (10,000 − 99,000)

Ten thousand till ninety nine thousand.

Seratus ribu hingga sejuta. (100 000 − 1 000 000)

One hundred thousand to one million.

Beberapa Contoh   Some Examples

Saya ada dua tangan dan sepuluh jari.

I have two hands and ten fingers.

Berapa mata anda?

How many eyes have you?

Saya ada dua biji mata. Saya ada sepasang mata.

I have two eyes. I have a pair of eyes.

Berapa umur anda?

How old are you?

Umur saya dua puluh lima tahun enam bulan.

I am twenty five years and six months old.

Saya tinggal empat belas kilometer dari sini.

I stay fourteen kilometres from here.

Harga buku ini lapan ringgit tiga puluh lima sen.

The price of this book is eight dollars and thirty five cents.

Perbendaharaan Kata　　Vocabulary　Part 2

kita	we
mesti	must
tahu	know
kira	count
mengira	to count
sebut	say
kemudian	then; after that
campur	increased by; plus
jadi	is; become
teruskan	continue; proceed
dapat	get
sampai	till
seterusnya	as we proceed
dapati	get
berapa	how many
dan	and
sepasang	a pair
umur	age
tinggal	live; stay
dari	from
sini	here
harga	cost; price

6

Penerangan   Explanations   Part 3

1. As mentioned in Lesson 5, **se** is a prefix commonly used to denote **one**, **a** or **an**; however its presence does not always represent **a** or **an**. For example, **selepas** = *after* and comes from the root word **lepas**.

    The same applies to **seterusnya** = as we proceed, further, in continuation. (It comes from the root word **terus**.)

2. **Dapat** means *get* while **dapati**, means *discovered* or *found*. eg

    i   **Saya *dapat* layanan baik.**

         I *got* (a) good reception.

    ii   **Saya *dapati* beg saya di rumah itu.**

         I *found* my bag in that house.

    iii **Saya cari buku, *terdapat* pensel.**

         I searched (for a) book (and) *found* (a) pencil.

    The English words in brackets are not expressed in Malay as they are understood, further evidence of the preciseness of Malay. The prefix **ter** when added to a verb expresses accidental completion of the action.

3. **Sepasang mata**, *Sepasang* is a classifier and means **a pair**. The use of classifiers is common in Malay and a few examples are given below.

    sebuah buku = **a** book (for large things)

    sebatang pen = **a** pen (for long rod-like things)

    dua **ekor** burung = two birds (for creatures)

    dua **orang** budak = two children (for humans)

    tiga **biji** telor = three eggs (for small round things).

PELAJARAN 7

PAKAIAN

LESSON 7   Part 1

CLOTHING

Orang di seluruh dunia memakai pakaian.

People all over the world wear clothes.

Ada banyak jenis pakaian.

There are many kinds of clothing.

Biasanya orang lelaki memakai kemeja dan seluar.

Usually men wear shirts and trousers.

Ada juga yang memakai tali leher.

There are some who wear a necktie.

Ramai orang memakai sarung kaki.

Many people wear socks.

Kita memakai kasut.

We wear shoes.

Ramai juga orang suka memakai selipar.

Many people too like to use slippers.

Orang perempuan biasanya memakai kain, skirt atau seluar.

Ladies usually wear **sarong** , skirts or slacks.

Mereka juga pakai baju kurung, kebaya atau blaus.

They also wear the **kurung, kebaya** or blouse.

Orang perempuan suka gunakan beg tangan.

Ladies like to use handbags.

Orang lelaki dan perempuan juga suka memakai tali pinggang.

Men and ladies also like to wear belts.

Kadang-kadang orang memakai sarung tangan dan baju panas.

Sometimes people wear gloves and a sweater.

Ramai orang membawa beg duit.

Many people carry purses.

Perbendaharaan Kata   Vocabulary   Part 2

orang	people
seluruh	all over
dunia	world
pakai	wear
ada	there is/are
ramai	many
jenis	types
biasanya	usually
orang lelaki	men

baju	shirt
seluar	trousers
juga	also; too
memakai	wear
tali leher	necktie
sarung kaki	socks
sarung kaki panjang	stockings
kasut	shoes
suka	like
selipar	slippers
orang perempuan	ladies
kain	the **sarong** (usually worn by Malay ladies)
seluar	slacks, pants
baju kurung	a National dress worn by Malay ladies
baju kebaya	a National dress, too, more tight-fitting than the *kurung*
gunakan	use
beg tangan	handbag
tali pinggang	belt
kadang-kadang	sometimes
sarung tangan	gloves
baju panas	sweater
membawa	carry or bring along
beg duit	purse

7

Penerangan   Explanations   Part 3

1. **Di (a place preposition) meaning** *at*, *in* or *on* is usually
    used to denote place.

    e.g. **Saya tinggal di sini.** (I live here.)

      Di mana buku? (Where is the book?)

2. **Pakaian** (from the verb **pakai**) can be used for both
    clothes and *clothing*.

3. Tali means string or rope. Used with nouns like *leher* (tali
    leher = necktie) and *pinggang* (tali pinggang = belt), it means
    something else, but retains some of its original meaning.

4. Note that some verbs can be converted to nouns by the
    addition of a suitable suffix, eg.

Verbs	Nouns
pakai (wear)	**pakaian** (clothes)
minum (drink)	**minuman** (drinks)
makan (eat)	**makanan** (food)

5. *Di* **as a Verbal Prefix**

    The prefix **di** may be attached to a simple verb to convert it
    into a passive verb.

      Bapa panggil Kassim.

    Father calls Kassim.

      Kassim dipanggil oleh bapa.

    Kassim was called by father.

    Note that the verb **dipanggil** is in the past tense and the
    preposition **by** (oleh) is followed by the doer of the action,
    (father).

Lelaki Muda	**Hari ini sejuk.**
	Today is a cold day.
Perempuan Muda	**Benar! Tetapi semalam hari panas.**
	That's right! But yesterday was a hot day.
Lelaki Muda	**Saya suka hari panas. Bagaimana anda?**
	I like a hot day. What about you?
Perempuan Muda	**Saya suka hari sejuk. Saya tidak suka hari panas.**
	I like a cold day. I do not like a hot day.
Lelaki Muda	**Jadi anda suka hujan tiap-tiap hari?**
	So you like it to rain everyday?

8

Perempuan Muda	**Tidak. Saya tidak suka hujan tiap-tiap hari.**
	No. I do not like it to rain everyday.
	Saya hanya suka hari sejuk.
	I only like a cold day.
Lelaki Muda	**Negeri kita negeri panas dan lembab.**
	Our country is hot and humid.
Perempuan Muda	**Benar. Tetapi saya sudah biasa sejuk.**
	That's right. But I am used to the cold.
	Saya datang dari negeri sejuk.
	I come from a cold country.
Lelaki Muda	**Saya tidak suka hari terlalu sejuk.**
	I do not like a very cold day.
Perempuan Muda	**Saya juga tidak suka hari terlalu sejuk atau terlalu panas.**
	I too do not like a very cold or a very hot day.
Lelaki Muda	**Negeri ini tidak mempunyai empat musim seperti negeri-negeri Barat.**
	This country does not have the four seasons like Western contries.
Perempuan Muda	**Ya. Negeri-negeri Barat ada musim bunga, musim panas, musim gugur dan musim salji.**
	Yes. Western countries have the seasons of spring, summer, autumn and winter.

Lelaki Muda	**Tentu seronok begitu.**
	That is pleasant.

Perbendaharaan Kata   Vocabulary   Part 2

sejuk	cold
benar	true; that's right
panas	hot
hujan	rain
tiap-tiap hari	everyday
hanya	only
negeri	country
lembab	humid
tetapi	but
biasa	used to
datang	come
terlalu	very
atau	or
mempunyai	have or has
musim	season
Barat	West
Musim Bunga	Spring
Musim Panas	Summer
Musim Gugur	Autumn
Musim Salji	Winter
tentu	sure; must be
seronok	pleasant; delightful
begitu	in that way

8

Penerangan   Explanations   Part 3

1. **Sejuk** may also mean *cool*.

   Tiap-tiap, *everyday*, may also be written **setiap**, e.g.

   Jadi awak suka hujan *setiap* **hari?**

   So you like it to rain everyday?

   Lembab, besides *humid*, may also mean *damp*.

   Kain ini masih lembab.

   This material is still damp.

2. Conjunctions or joining words include:

   dan − and

   tetapi − but

   atau − or

3. The word **musim** (season) is used with the following
   other words:

musim panas	season when flowers appear
musim hujan	rainy season
musim panas	hot season

4. *Ya* and *Tidak*

   A question can be affirmed by saying **ya** (yes). Negation is
   expressed by **tidak** (no, not). Often a relevant word from the
   question is repeated to avoid impolite abruptness in the reply.

Mereka sudah makan?	Have they eaten?
Ya, sudah.	Yes, (they) have.
Tidak, belum lagi.	No, not yet.

Ada banyak jenis buah-buahan.

There are many kinds of fruits.

Ada buah-buahan tempatan dan luar negeri.

There are local and foreign fruits.

Buah-buahan tempatan banyak datangnya dari Malaysia.

Many local fruits come from Malaysia.

Contoh buah-buahan tempatan ialah pisang, betik, durian, nenas, manggis, rambutan dan banyak jenis lagi.

Examples of local fruits are bananas, papayas, durians, pineapples, mangosteens, rambutans and many more.

9

Ada buah yang mempunyai biji.

Some fruits have seeds.

Ini termasuk rambutan, durian dan manggis.

These include rambutans, durians and mangosteens.

Misalan buah-buahan luar negeri ialah epal, limau, anggor dan per.

Examples of foreign fruits are apples, oranges, grapes and pears.

Buah-buahan ada yang kecil dan besar.

There are small and large fruits.

Buah-buahan juga berwarna-warni.

Fruits too are colourful.

Ada yang merah, ada yang hijau, ada yang kuning dan lain-lain warna lagi.

Some are red, some are green, some are yellow and others are of many other colours.

Setengah buah-buahan mempunyai kulit yang tidak boleh dimakan.

Some fruits have skins that cannot be eaten.

Ini termasuk pisang, betik, durian dan nenas.

These include bananas, papayas, durians and pineapples.

Ada buah-buahan mempunyai kulit yang boleh dimakan.

Some fruits have skins that can be eaten.

Ini termasuk anggur dan per.

These include grapes and pears.

Buah-buahan mengandungi zat-zat, gula dan air.

Fruits contain vitamins, sugar and water.

Buah-buahan baik untuk kesihatan.

Fruits are good for health.

Perbendaharaan Kata   Vocabulary   Part 2

buah	fruit
buah-buahan	fruits
tempatan	local
luar negeri	foreign
contoh; misalan	examples
mempunyai	have
biji	seed/s
termasuk	include
kecil	small
besar	big
berwarna-warni	colourful
merah	red
hijau	green
kuning	yellow
dan lain-lain lagi	and many others
setengah	some
kulit	skin
dimakan	eaten
mengandungi	contain
zat	vitamin
zat-zat	vitamins
gula	sugar
air	water

9

baik	good
untuk	for
kesihatan	health
pisang	banana
betik	papaya
durian	durian
nanas	pineapple
manggis	mangosteen
rambutan	rambutan
epal	apple
limau	orange
anggur	grape
per	pear

Penerangan   Explanations   Part 3

1. **Tempatan** meaning *local* comes from the word **tempat** meaning *place*.
2. **Buah** means *a fruit*; **buah-buah** is the plural form. **Buah-buahan** means *a variety of fruits*.
3. **Biji** means *seed*; **biji-biji** is *seeds*. But **biji-bijian** means *cereal(s)*.

    Biji is also used as a classifier for small objects, e.g.

sebiji epal	one/an apple
dua biji limau	two oranges
beberapa biji per	several pears

PELAJARAN 10

MEMBELI-BELAH

LESSON 10　Part 1

SHOPPING

Lelaki Muda	**Apa kata kalau kita pergi membeli-belah?**
	How about going shopping?
Perempuan Muda	**Tentu sekali boleh.**
	Most certainly.
Lelaki Muda	**Sekarang ada banyak jual-murah di kedai-kedai.**
	There are many 'cheap sales' in the shops.
Perempuan Muda	**Apa yang anda hendak beli?**
	What do you want to buy?

10

Lelaki Muda	**Saya hendak beli dua helai kemeja dan sepasang sepatu.**
	I want to buy two shirts and a pair of shoes.
Perempuan Muda	**Saya hendak beli sehelai baju.**
	I want to buy a dress.
Lelaki Muda	**Mari kita bersiap dan pergi cepat.**
	Let's get ready and go quickly.
Perempuan Muda	**Lihat, kedai itu sangat sesak.**
	See, that shop is very packed.
Lelaki Muda	**Ya, mari kita ke kedai sebelah.**
	Yes, let's go to the next shop.
Perempuan Muda	**Cuba lihat kemeja ini. Cantik betul!**
	Look at this shirt. It's beautiful!
Lelaki Muda	**Ya, pandai anda memilihnya. Saya akan belinya.**
	Yes, you're clever at choosing. I shall buy it.
Perempuan Muda	**Saya akan tolong anda cari saiznya.**
	I'll help you to find the right size.
Lelaki Muda	**Yang ini pun cantik dan saiznya pun tepat.**
	This one too is beautiful and its size, too, is just right.

Perempuan Muda	**Anda beruntung, sudah pun dapat dua helai kemeja!**
	You're lucky, having found your two shirts!
Lelaki Muda	**Sekarang mari kita cari baju anda.**
	Now, let's find your dress.
Perempuan Muda	**Nampaknya baju-baju di kedai ini tidak begitu cantik**
	Looks like the dresses in this shop aren't that beautiful.
Lelaki Muda	**Mari kita ke kedai lain.**
	Let's go to another shop.
Perempuan Muda	**Bagaimana dengan baju ini, cantik tak?**
	How about this dress, beautiful isn't it?
Lelaki Muda	**Sangat cantik. Anda pandai benar memilih!**
	Very beautiful. You are really good at choosing!
Perempuan Muda	**Harganya pun tidak begitu mahal. Saya akan ambilnya.**
	Its price too is not very expensive. I'll take it.
Lelaki Muda	**Saya sudah penat. Saya akan beli kasut saya pada lain masa.**
	I'm already tired. I shall buy my shoes some other time.

10

Perempuan Muda **Mari kita pulang ke rumah.**

Let's go home.

Perbendaharaan Kata   Vocabulary Part 2

apa kata	how about...?
kalau	if
kita	we
pergi	go
membeli-belah	shopping
tentu sekali	most certainly
boleh	can
sekarang	now
jual-murah	sale; cheap sale
kedai-kedai	shops
hendak	want
beli	buy
helai	numeral coefficient for cloth, shirt, dress, etc
sepasang	a pair
bersiap	get ready
cepat	fast; quickly
lihat	see
sesak	packed; conjested
mari	come; let's go
sebelah	next door
cuba	please
cantik betul	really beautiful

pandai	clever
memilihnya	to choose it
akan	will; shall
tolong	help; assist
cari	to find
saiz	size
tepat	just right; exact
beruntung	having luck
sudah	already
lain	another
harganya	its price
mahal	expensive
ambil	take
penat	tired
lain masa	next time; some other time
pulang	go back (home)
rumah	house; home

Penerangan   **Explanations   Part 3**

1. **Helai** can be equated to the word *piece;* it is used as a classifier for *cloth, dress,* etc. e.g.

sehelai kain	a piece of sarong/cloth
sehelai belaus	a blouse
tiga helai baju	three shirts.

2. **Cuba** means *try;* it can also be used courteously to mean *please.*

   e.g. **Anda mesti** *cuba* **lagi.**   You must *try* again.
   Cuba **lihat burung**   (Please) look at that
   itu.   bird.

3. **Betul** means *right* or *correct.*; however when prefixed with another word it brings about an emphasis, e.g.

cantik betul   (it's) really beautiful

baik betul   really good

Cuba lihat: nakal betul budak itu!

Just look: that child is really mischievous!

4. **Tenses**

The present, past and future tenses are identifiable in Malay.

i   **Present Tense (Continuous Action)**

To express the *present continuous tense* expressed in English by words like *while, still, am* and *in the midst of,* the Malay word **sedang** is used before the verb.

Bapa *sedang* menulis surat.

Father is (still) writing (a) letter.

Sedang berjalan, dia pengsan.

While walking, he fainted.

ii   **Present Tense**

Saya berjalan.   I am walking.

Ahmad menulis surat. Ahmad is writing/writes a letter.

iii   **Past Tense**

It is expressed by the use of the words **telah** or **sudah** (less formal) before the verb.

Hassan telah balik ke rumah.

Hassan (has) returned to (his) house.

iv   **Future Tense**
The word **akan** is used before the verb to express the future tense.
Emak akan datang besok.
Mother will come tomorrow.

Index on Points of Grammar

The first digit indicates the **Lesson** No. and the digit that follows (within brackets) refers to the paragraph No. of the **Explanations** section of that Lesson.

MALAY-ENGLISH DICTIONARY

A

aba father
abadi everlasting, without end
abang elder brother
acar pickled vegetables
acara programme
ada have, has, there is, are
adab manners
adalat justice
adib polite
adik younger brother or sister
afiat healthy
agak guess
agak baik quite well
agama religion
agung grand, great, highest
Ahad Sunday
ahli member of an association
air water
air terjun waterfall
air wangi perfume
aja only
ajaib strange
ajakan invitation
ajar teach, instruct
akad promise
akal idea, plan
akan will, shall
akar root
akhbar news
akibat result, outcome
akil clever
akmal perfect
aku I, me, my
akuran tally
alam world, earth
alamat address
alat tool, instrument
alat ukur measuring device
alim learned, pious
alis eye brow
Allah God
almari cupboard

amah maid, servant
aman peaceful, calm
amaran warning
amat very
ambil take, fetch
ampu big toe, thumb
ampun forgiveness, pardon
anak child
anak saudara nephew or niece
anda you, your
anggaran estimate
anggur grapes
angin wind, air in motion
angka figure
angkat lift, raise
angsa goose
anih strange, odd, unusual
anjing dog
antara between; in the middle of
 two things
antarabangsa international
apa how; in what way
apa-apa whatever
apabila when, whenever
apakala when
apa kata how about ...?
apa lagi what more, what else
api fire
arak liquor
arang charcoal
arnab rabbit
asa hope
asal beginning
asam sour
asap smoke
asas foundation
asli original
asmara love, adoration
aspek aspect
asrama hostel
asyik infatuated
atap roof
atas on top (of)
atau or

awak you
awal early
awan cloud
awas beware, caution
ayah father
ayam hen fowl
ayat sentence
ayim contented

B

bacaan reading
badam almond
bagaimana how
bagi give
bah flood
bahasa language
bahaya danger
bahu shoulder(s)
baik good
baik sedikit a little better
baja fertilizer
baju shirt
baju kebaya a national dress more tight-fitting than the kurung
baju kurung a national dress worn by Malay ladies
baju panas sweater
baki balance
bakul basket
balai hall, station, kiosk
baldi pail
balik return
bandar large and important town
bangku bench
bangsa nationality
bangun get up; stand
bantal pillow
bantuan aid
banyak many
bapa father
bapa engkat foster father
bapa saudara uncle
barang thing

barat west
baru just, new
basah wet
batal cancel
batu stone
bau odour
bawah under
bawang onion
bayar pay, give
bazir waste
bebas free
beg bag
beg duit purse
begini like this
begitu in that way
beg tangan handbag
bekerja work
belajar learn, study
belakang back
belanja spend
beli buy
belok bend, curve
belum not yet
benar true; that's right
benci hate
benda things
bengkok crooked
bentuk figure
beranak bear a child
berani brave
berapa how many
beras uncooked rice
berat heavy
berat telinga hard of hearing
berasa feel
berempat the four (of us)
bergerak move
berhampiran nearby; not far from
berjumpa to visit, to consult
beri give
berita news
benafas breathe
bersama with
bersiap get ready

bersih clean
beruntung having luck
berwarna-warni colourful
besar big
betik papaya
betina female
betul true
biasa used to
biasanya usually
bibir lip
bijak clever
biji seed/s
bil bill
bila when
bilik room
bilik bacaan reading room
bilik serbaguna multipurpose room
bimbang worried
binatang animal
bintang star
biro bureau
biru blue
bisa poison
bising noisy
bisu dumb
bocor leak
bodoh stupid
bogel naked
bohong false
bola ball
boleh can, may
bomoh Malay medicine man
bonda mother
botak bald
botol bottle
buah-buahan fruits
buang throw
budak young child
buka open
bukan not, no
bukit hill
bukti proof
buku book
buku lali ankle

bunga flower
bunuh kill
bunyi sound
buruk ugly
burung bird
buta blind

C

cabai chillie
cabang branch
cabut uproot; flee
cacar smallpox, restless
cacau confused
cacing worm
cadar bed sheet
cahaya light
cair liquid
cakar claw
calun candidate
campak throw down
campur mix, combine; increased by; plus
cangkul hoe
cantik pretty
cantik betul really beautiful
cara way, method
cari to find, look for
cat paint
cawan cup, small bowl
cawangan branch, division
cebong tadpole
cedera hurt, injured
cek cheque
celak mascara
celaka bad
cemburu jealous
cencang chop
cendawan mushroom
cenderong sloping
cepat fast; quickly
cerah bright, clear
cerai separate
ceramah speech, lecture

cerdas intelligent, alert
cerdik clever, intelligent
cerek kettle
cerewet fussy
cergas fast
cerita story
cermat careful
cermin mirror
cerut cigar
cicak lizard
cikgu teacher
cincin ring
cinta love
comel pretty, beautiful
contoh; misalan sample; examples
cuaca weather
cuba please
cuba-cuba trial and error
cuci wash
cucu grandchild
cukai tax
cukup enough
cukur shave
cuma only
curi steal
cuti leave

D

dada chest
dadah drugs
dadih curdled milk
daerah district
daftar register
daftaran enrolment
daging meat
dagu chin
dahaga thirsty
dahi forehead
dahsyat frightening
dahulu past
dakwat ink
dalam in, deep
damai peace

dan and
dan lain-lain lagi and many others
dapat get
dapati get
dapur kitchen
darah blood
darat land
dari from
daripada from
darjah class
datang arrive, come
datuk grandfather
daun leaf
dawai wire
degil stubborn
dekat near
demam fever
denda punishment, fine
dendam revenge
dengan with (preposition)
dengar hear
depan front
deras fast
derma donation
dewasa adult
di at, in
di mana where
dia he, she
diam silent
digunakan is used (passive voice)
dimakan eaten
dinding wall
dingin cold, chilly
diri self, one's own
disebut is referred to
doa prayer
dobi dhobi
doktor physician, doctor
dompet wallet
dondang song sung for enjoyment
dosa sin
dua two
duabelas twelve
dua puluh twenty

duduk sit
duit money
duka grief
dukacita sorrow, feeling regret
dukun village medicine man
dulang tray
dunia world
duri thorn
durian durian
dusun orchard

E

ekor tail
ela yard
elaun allowance
elok good
emak mother
emak saudara aunty
emas gold
embun dew
empat four
emper verandah
emping rice cooked before it has attained maturity
enak delicious as of taste
enak hati contented
enam six
enam puluh sixty
encik mister
enek feeling sick, nauseated
engkau you, your
enjin engine
entah an expression of doubt
epal apple
erti meaning
esa one, sole
esah legal, legitimate
esei essay
esok tomorrow

F

fadil prominent

faedah good use
faham understand
fail file
fajar dawn
fakta fact
famili family
fasal paragraph
fasih fluent
feri ferry
fesyen fashion
fikir think
filem film
firdaus paradise
firma firm
fitnah libel
fitrah tithe
foto photograph

G

gadai pawn
gadis maiden
gaduh quarrel
gaduk arrogant
gagal fail
gajah elephant
gaji salary, wages
galah forked pole
gali dig
gambar picture
ganas ferocious, fierce
ganggu disturb
gangsa bronze
ganja hemp plant used as narcotic drug
ganjil strange
gantang measure of capacity
ganti substitute
gantung hang
gaok crow
gapit tweezers, pincers
garam salt
garang fierce, ferocious
garing crisp

garis draw a line
garpu fork
garu scratch
gasing top
gatal itchy
gaul mix
gaya conduct, bearing
gedung store
gelak laugh
gelang bangle
gelap dark
geledek thunder
geletar tremble, shiver
gelip twinkle
gelisah worried
gelisar restless
gemar fond
gembira very happy
Gemelan jawanese orchestra
gementar vibrate
gempa tremor
gemuk fat
gerai stall
geram angry, annoyed
gereja church
gergaji saw
gergasi giant
ghaib disappear
giat active
gigi tooth or teeth
gigit bite
gila mad
giliran turn
goreng fry
gosok scrub
gua cave
gudang warehouse
gula sugar
gulai food with gravy
guli marble
gulung roll
guna use
gunakan use (active voice)
guni sack

gunting scissors
gunung mountain
guru teacher
gurun desert
gusi gums
gusti wrestle

H

habis without any remaining
had limit
hadapan front
hadiah gift
hadir present
hafal memorize
haiwan animals other than man
hajat wish
haji man who has made pilgrimage
  to Mecca
hak right
hakim judge
hal situation
halal permissible according to
  Islamic laws
halaman compound
halau drive away
halia ginger
halus fine
hamba slave
hamil pregnant
hampir near
hancur crushed
hangat hot, warm
hangit smell of burning cloth or rice
hangus burnt
hantar to send
hantu evil spirit
hanya only
hapus disappear
harga cost; price
harganya its price
hari day, time between sunrise &
  sunset
hari-hari every; daily

57

hari ini today
harimau tiger
harta property
harum sweet smelling
hasil earnings
hasrat longing
hati liver
haus thirsty
hawa air
hayat life
hebat terrible
helai piece
henti stop
hidung nose
hidup live, alive
hijau green
hikmat knowledge, wisdom
hilang lost
himpun gather
hingga until
hisap suck up
hitam black
hormat respect
hujan rain
hukum sentence
huruf letter of alphabet
hutan jungle
hutang debt, loan

iklan advertisement
iklim climate
ikrab intimate
ikut follow
ilham divine inspiration
ilmu knowledge
imam leader of prayer in a group
iman faith
inai henna
indah beautiful
ingat remember
ingin long for
ini this
Injil Bible
insaf aware
insan mortal man
intan diamond
inti filling
irama tempo, beat
isap suck, inhale
isi flesh meat or fruit
Isnin Monday
istana palace
isteri wife
istiadat custom
isyarat signal
itik duck
itu that

I

ia it
iaitu that is
ialah is
ianya its
iblis the devil
ibu mother
ibu dan bapa parents
idap eyelash
ijazah diploma
ikan fish
ikat tie up
ikhlas sincere
ikhtiar free choice

J

jadi is, become
jadikan; menjadi make
jadual list
jaga alert, awake
jagung maize, corn
jahanam hell
jahat bad, evil
jahil ignorant
jahit sew
jala casting net for catching fish
jalan a road
jalat nauseated
jam hour, clock

jamban lavatory, toilet
jambatan bridge
jambu guava, a type of fruit
jambul turf of hair on head
jamin guarantee
jampi incantation
jamu entertain
jana life
janda widow, divorcee
jangan don't, do not
janggut beard
janji promise
jantan male
jantina sex
jantung heart
jarang seldom, rarely
jari kaki toes
jari tangan fingers
jasmani physical
jatuh fall, drop
jauh far
jawab answer, reply
jaya win
jel jail
jelak fed up, bored
jelas clear of words, view
jelewat fresh water fish
jeling give a side long look
jelita beautiful, charming
jembrut emerald
jemput invite
jemu bored
jemur dry in the sun
jenaka funny, comical
jenayah criminal, crime
jenazah corpse
jendela window
jenis type, kind
jentera wheel, machine
jeram rapid
jerat trap, snare
jerawat pimple, acne
jerit scream
jika if, on condition

jikalau if, supposing that
jilat lap, lick
jimat thrifty
jinak tame
jiran neighbour
jiwa life, spirit, soul
jodoh match
joget type of dance
johan champion
jual sell
jual-murah sale; cheap sale
juara champion, expert in certain field
juaran fishing rod
judi gambling
juga also
jujur honest, trustworthy
juling cross eyed
Jumaat Friday
jumlah total
jumpa meet
juru expert, specialist
jurutera engineer
juta million
jutawan millionaire

K

Kaabah cube like stone found in Mecca
kabab small pieces of meat roasted on a spit
kabul agreed
kabus haze
kaca glass
kacak handsome
kacang nut, bean
kacau disturb, annoy
kadang-kadang sometimes
kadi judge in Muslim matters
kah suffix expressing a question
kahwin marry, wed
kain cloth, sarong (worn by Malay ladies)

kajicuaca meteorology, science of the weather
kakak elder sister
kakaktua cockatoo
kakanda polite form for elder sister
kaki leg
kakitangan worker, helper
kalah lost, defeated
kalau if
kaldai donkey
kali multiply
kalung necklace
kamar room
kambing goat
kami we (including speaker)
kampung village, country side
kamu you, your
kamus dictionary
kanak child
kanan right
kancil mousedeer
kandung fill with
kanun laws
kapak axe
kapal ship
kapalterbang aeroplane
kapas cotton
kapur cotton
kapur limestone
karang soon, later, afterwards
karat rust
karma all the actions of person throughout his life on earth
kasar thick, coarse
kasih love
kasihan pity
kasut shoes
kata spoken word or words
katak frog
katil bed
kau you
kaum group
kawan friend
kaya rich

kayu wood
ke to, towards (direction)
ke sana there
kebas paralysed
kebun garden
kecil small
keciwa disappointed
kecuali except
kedai shop
kehendak wish
kejar chase
keju cheese
kejut shock, surprise
kelapa coconut
klinik clinic
keluar go or move outside
keluarga family, parents and children
kemas tidy
kembali return, once more
kembar twins
kemeja shirt
kemudian later, then
kena hit, strike
kenal recognize
kenapa why
kenduri feast
kepala head
kepala lutut knee-cap
keping piece
kerana because
kerani clerk
kereta vehicle
keretapi train
kering dry
kerja work
kerjaya career
kertas paper
kerusi chair
kesihatan health
ketam crab
ketat tight
ketawa laugh
ketua chief, leader

ketuk knock
ketupat rice cooked in woven
   coconut leave
khabar news
Khamis Thursday
khas special
khayal fantasy
khazanah possessions
khidmat serve, work
kicap brown sauce made from soya
   bean
kilang factory
kilat lightning
kini now
kipas fan
kira count
kiri left
kirim deliver
kita we (including speaker)
kongsi share, combine
korban sacrifice
kosong empty
kotak box
kotor dirty
kuali frying pan
kuasa power
kuat strong
kuatkuasa authority
kubur grave, tomb
kucing cat
kuda horse
kudis sores
kuih cake
kuku nail (of finger of toes)
kukus steam
kulit skin
kuman germs
kunci lock
kuning yellow colour
kupu-kupu butterfly
kurang insufficient
kursus course
kurus thin
kutu louse flea

L

labu gourd
laci drawer
lada pepper
ladang field farm
lagi more
lagu intonation, song
lahir create, to be born
lain other, another
lain masa next time
laju rapid, fast
laki husband
laku demand, can be sold
lalat fly
lalu walk past
lama former, past
lambat slow, late
lampin baby's napkin
lampu lamp
langgar collide, clash
langit sky
langsir curtain
langsung forthwith
lap mop, wipe
lapan eight
lapar hungry
lapis layer
lapur report
lari run
laut sea
layak qualified
layan wait on
layang-layang kite
layar sail
layu withered
lazat delicious
lebar wide, broad
lebat thick
lebih more, greater
leher neck (front)
lekas quick, fast
lekat stick to
lelah fatigued, tired

lelaki muda young man
lemah weak
lemak fat
lemang glutinous rice cooked in
  bamboo
lemas suffocating
lembab humid
lembaga board, committee
lembu cow
lembut soft
lena deep, profound
lengan arm
lengar dizzy
lengkap exact, complete
lenyap disappear, vanish
lepas free
letak position, site
letih tire, weary
lewat over, finished
liar wild
licin smooth
lidah tongue
lihat see
lilin wax
lima five
lima puluh fifty
limau orange, lemon
lintas pass, cross
lipas cockroach
lisan words, speech
loceng bell
lompat jump
longgar loose
lorong lane
luar outside
luarbiasa unusual
luar negeri foreign
luas broad, wide
lubang hole
lubang hidung nostrils
lucu funny
ludah saliva, spit
luka wound, hurt
lukis draw

lupa forget
lurus straight
lusa day after tomorrow
lutut knee

M

maaf forgiveness, pardon
mabuk drunk
macam kind, type
macis matches
madu nectar, sweet liquid in flowers
mahal expensive
maharaja great king, emperor
maharani queen
mahasiswa university student
mahkamah court
mahkota crown
mahu want, desire
main play
majalah magazine
majikan employer
majlis council
maju advance, go forward
mak abbreviated form of mother
makan eat
makanan food
makan tengahari lunch
makan malam dinner
makcik aunt
maki scold
maklumat announcement
makmal laboratory
makna meaning
maksud wish, intention
maktab college
malam night
malang unlucky
malu shy
mampu able
mana where, how
mandang stare at
mandi bathe
mangga padlock

manggis mangosteen
mangkuk bowl
mangsa prey
manis sweet
manja pampered
manusia human being
marah angry
mari come here
mas gold
masa time
masalah matter
masak ripe
masam sour
masih still
masuk enter
masyarakat society
masyhur famous
mata eye or eyes
matahari sun
mati dead
mayat corpse
medan field
meja table
melalui through
melewatkan to delay
melihat see
memang of course, naturally
memakai wear
memandu drive, to control vehicle
membawa carry or bring along
membeli-belah shopping
memilihnya to choose it
mempunyai own, possess (verb)
  have or has
menang victorious
menantu son-in-law
mencium smell
mendengar to hear
mendung cloudy or overcast
mengandungi contain
mengangkat carry
mengira to count
mentah unripe
mentega butter

menteri minister
merah red colour
merasa taste
merdeka independent, free
mereka they
mesti must, should
mimpi dream
minggu week
minit minutes
minta ask for, request
minyak oil
misal example
miskin poor
mogok strike
mohon ask, apply
muda young
mudah easy, simple
muka face
mula beginning, start
mulut mouth
murah cheap
musim season
musim bunga spring
musim gugur autumn
musim panas summer
musim salji winter
musnah destroyed
mustahak important
mustahil impossible
musuh enemy
mutiara pearl
mutu quality

N

nafas breath
nafsu desire
naga dragon
nahas unlucky
naik ascend, climb
nakal mischievous
nama name
nampak see, observe
nanti wait

nasi cooked rice
nasib fortune, destined
nasihat advice
Natal Christmas
negara country
nelayan fisherman
nenas pineapple
nenek grandmother
neraka hell
niat aim, intention
nikah wedding
nikmat delight, satisfaction
nilai value
nipis thin
nirmala pure, clean
nirwana state of bliss
nya his, her, its
nyamuk mosquito
nyawa life, soul
nyonya term used for a woman who
   is not a Malay

O

Ogos August
olah method
oleh by
ombak wave
opah grandfather
orang people
orang gaji servant
orang lelaki men
orang perempuan ladies
oren orange
otak brains
otak-otak food made out of fish
otot muscle
oyong swinging, swaying

P

pada at, in, on
padam extinguished
padang field

padi pearl white grain
pagar fence
pagi morning
paha thigh
pahlawan warrior
pajak pawn
pakai wear
pakar expert
pakcik uncle
paksa force
paku nail
paling very, extremely
panas hot
pancaragam band
pancing fish
pandai clever
pandang look, stare
panggil call, summon
panggung stage, platform
pangkat rank
panjang long
papan plank, board
paraf initials
parai bitter gourd
parang chopper
parit drain, channel
paru-paru lungs
pasang pair, assemble
pasar market
pasir sand
pasti undoubted, sure
pasu vase, pot
pasukan team
patah broken
patari solder
patung image, statue
patut proper, suitable
pawang magician
payung umbrella
pecah smash, break
pedas spicy, hot
pedih smarting
pedu gall
peduli care, heed

pegang hold, grasp
pegawai officer
peguam lawyer
peha thigh
pejabat office
pekak deaf
pekan town
pekat thick
pelabuhan port, harbour
peladang farmer
pelajar pupil, student
pelajaran lesson
pelakun actor
pelancung tourist
pelangi rainbow
pelawat visitor
pelayan waiter
pelihara rear
peluh sweat
peluk hug, embrace
pelukis artist
peluru bullet
pembaris ruler
penari dancer
penat tired
pencuri thief
pendek short
pengantin bride or bridegroom
pengarah director
pengarang author
pengecut coward
penghulu headman
pengsan fainted
pening dizzy
penjara prison
pentas stage
penting important
penuh full
penyakit disease
penyapu broom
per pear
perabot furniture
perang war
percaya believe

percuma without payment
perdana prime
perempuan muda young girl
pergelangan tangan wrist
pergi go
periksa inspect
peringkat grade
perintah command
perkara affair, matter
perlahan slowly
perli tease
perlu must, ought to
permata gem
pernah ever
pertama first
pertanian agriculture
perut stomach
pesta carnival
petang afternoon; evening
peti chest box with lid
piala trophy
pijak step, tread
pilihanraya election
pinggan plate
pinggang waist
pinjam borrow
pintu door
pipi cheek
piring saucer
pisang banana
pisau knife
pokok tree
pondok hut
potong cut
puas satisfied
puasa fast, abstain
pucat pale
puji praise
pujuk coax
pukul hit, beat, time
pula again
pulang return
pulau island
pun also

punggung buttocks
punya own, have
pusat navel
pusing rotate
putera prince
putih white colour
putus broken

Q

Quran the Koran

R

Rabu Wednesday
racun poison
rahsia secret
rakan friend
rakyat citizen
ramai plenty
rambut hair
rambutan rambutan
rantai chain
rapat close
rasa taste
rasmi official
ratu queen
ratus hundred
raya important, great
rempah spice
rencana article, feature
rendah low
rendam soak
rendang fried
ria gay, lively
riang very happy, joyous
ribu thousand
ribut gale
rimba forest
rindu yearn
ringgit dollar
risau worried
roda wheel
rogol rape

roh soul
rokok cigarette
ronda patrol
rontok fall
rosak damaged
roti bread
ruang space
rugi loss
rumah house, home
rumah sakit hospital
rumput grass
runcit various kinds
runtuh collapse
rupa appearance

S

sabar patient
Sabtu Saturday
sabun soap
sah legal
sahabat friend
sahaja only
saham share
saiz size
sakit ill, unwell, pain
sakit kepala headache
saksi witness
saku pocket
salah wrong
salam greetings
salin change
sama alike
sambung lengthen
sampah rubbish
sampai till
sana there
sangat very
sangkut hang
santan coconut milk
sarapan breakfast
sarung kaki socks
sarung kaki panjang stockings
sarung tangan gloves

satu one
saya I
sayang love
sayur vegetable
sebab because
sebelah next door
sebulan a month
sebut say
sedang word expressing continuous
action
sedang bekerja working
sedap delicious
sedar conscious
sederhana moderate
sedia ready
sedih sad
sedikit little
segan shy
segera fast
sehari a day
sejuk cold
sekali once
sekarang now
sekolah school
selalu always
selama while
selamat safe
selamat jalan goodbye
selamat pagi good morning
selamat tinggal greeting to someone
staying behind
Selasa Tuesday
selera appetite
selesai finished
selimut blanket
selindang scarf
selipar slippers
seluar trousers, pants, slacks
seluruh all over
sembahyang pray
sementara temporary
seminggu a week
sempit narrow
semua all

semula again
semut ant
senang easy
sendiri own self
sentiasa always
senyap silent
senyum smile
seorang alone, one person
sepanjang full
sepasang pair
sepupu cousin (male or female)
serbuk powder, dust
seronok pleasant, enjoyable
sesak packed, congested
sesuai matching, suitable
setahun a year
setengah some
seterusnya as we proceed
sewa rent
sial unlucky
siang day-time
siap ready
siapa who, whose (pronoun) used
only for persons
sibuk busy
sihat healthy
sijil certificate
sikat comb
siku elbow
sila please
silap mistaken
simpan keep
sini here
soal question
songket cloth which is embroidered
with gold or silver threads
suami husband
suara voice
sudah completed, already
suka happy
sukan sports
sulit secret
sungai river
sungguh time, exact

sunyi quiet
surat letter
susah difficult
susu milk

T

taat obedient, loyal
tabung money box
tadi just now
tahan lasting
tahniah congratulations
tahu know
tahun year
tajam sharp
tak akan will not, having no
   intention to
tak mengapa don't worry, that's all
   right
takdir divine will
takut afraid
tali string, rope
tali leher necktie
tali pinggang belt
taman garden
tamat end
tampal patch
tanah land
tanda mark
tanduk horn
tangan hand
tangga steps
tangkap catch, seize
tanpa without
tapak kaki sole of foot
tapak tangan palm
tapis fitter, strain
tarik pull
tarikh date
tebal thick
tebu sugarcane
teguh firm, strong
telah did, has
telan swallow

telinga ear(s)
telur egg
teman friend
tembak shoot
temberang nonsense
tempat place
tempatan local
temu meet
temuduga interview
tenaga energy
tengah centre
tengah hari midday, noon
tengah malam midnight
tenggelam sink
tengkuk nape of neck
tentera army
tentu sure, must be
tentu sekali most certainly
tepat just right, exact
tepung flour
terang bright, clear
terbang fly
terbenam sets (of the sum)
terbit rises, appears (of the sun)
terima receive
terimakasih thank you
terjun jump
terlalu very
termasuk include
teruskan continue, proceed
tetap permanent
tetapi but
tiap-tiap hari everyday
tidak (tak) not, no
tidur sleep
tilam mattress
timun cucumber
timur east
tinggal stay, live
tinggi tall
tingkap window
tipu lie, cheat
tirai curtain
tolak push

tolong help, assist
tua old
tuan sir, mister
tudung cover, hid
tugas duty, task
tukang luak second hand dealer
tukang tinju boxer
tukar exchange
tukuk add
tukul hammer
tulang bone
tular inject, contaminate
tuli deaf
tulin pure
tulis write
tumbak spear
tumbuh grow, sprout
tumbuk box
tumis fry
tumpah spill
tumpat filled to the brim
tumpul blunt
tunang fiance
tunas shoot, bud, sprout
tunda tow
tunduk bow down the head
tunggu wait, keep watch
tunjuk point at, show, display
turun descend
tutup close
tutup mulut shut one's mouth
tutur talk, utterance

U

ubah change, alter
ubat medicine
ucap speak, talk
ucap selamat greetings
udara air
ugama religion
ukur measure
ulang repeat
ular snake

ulat worm
umur age, life
umurnya his/her age
undang-undang law
unta camel
untuk for
upacara rite, ceremony
upah fee, wages
urat vein
urus organise
urut massage
usik disturb
utama main
utang debt
utara north

V

varia variety
visi view

W

wajar natural, justified
wajib duty-bound
wakil representative
waktu time
walau although
wali person who can give away a bride
wang money
wangi fragrant
wanita woman
warganegara citizen
waris heir
warna colour
warta news, report
wartawan reporter, journalist
warung stall
wasiat will
wau paper kite
wayang plays or shows
wilayah district

X

x-ray x-ray, form of short wave ray

Y

ya answer to something in the affirmative
ya yes
yakin confident
yang which, who, that
yatim child whose parents are dead
yayasan fund
yunit unit, thing or group
yuran fee

Z

zakat Muslim tithe payable after the fasting month
zalim cruel
zaman period, time
zamindar land owner
zamrud emerald
zat vitamins, essence of food
zat-zat vitamins
zinah adultery
zirafah giraffe
Zohor afternoon prayers

NOTES

NOTES

LIST OF SIMPLE BOOK-CASSETTES

1	Simple Arabic	9	Simple Korean
2	Bahasa Arab	10	Simple Mandarin
3	Simple English (1)*	11	Simple Thai
4	Simple English (2)	12	Simple Tamil
5	Simple English (3)	13	Simple French
6	Simple Indonesian	14	Simple German
7	Simple Malay	15	Simple Spanish
8	Simple Japanese	16	Simple Italian

* Translations in: (1) Malay (2) Mandarin (3) Japanese

ABOUT THE BOOK-CASSETTES

Cassette

A Book-Cassette comprises a **Simple** language book and a 60 minute cassette which contains the recording of **ten** Lessons in the native language. Each sentence or phrase is followed by a **pause** for the learner to speak in imitation of the teacher. This provides essential **practice** in the spoken language.

Book

The book contains the same ten Lessons as in the cassette. Each Lesson has its **Vocabulary List** and Explanations of **grammar** to help the students construct his own sentences for meaningful conversations.

Delivery

A Book-Cassette comprising a book of about **100 pages**, a **60** minute cassette of recordings and surface mail postage including packing is **S$79**. Please add **S$26** if air mail delivery is required.

LIST OF BASIC BOOK-CASSETTES

1	Basic English (1)*	6	Basic Hindi
2	Basic English (2)	7	Basic Hokkien
3	Basic Thai	8	Basic Vietnamese
4	Basic Japanese	9	Basic Cantonese
5	Basic Filipino		

* Translations in: (1) Malay (2) Mandarin

ABOUT THE BOOK-CASSETTES

Cassettes

A Book-Cassettes comprises a **Basic** language book and two cassettes which contain the recording ot **ten** to **fifteen** Lessons in the foreign language. Each sentence or phrase is followed by a **pause** for the learner to speak in imitation of the teacher. This provides essential **practice** in the spoken language.

Book

The book contains the same ten to fifteen Lessons as in the cassettes. Each Lesson has its **Vocabulary List** and Explanations of **grammar** to help the student construct his own sentences for meaningful conversations.

Delivery

A Book-Cassettes comprising a book of about **130 pages**, two cassettes of recordings and surface mail postage including packing is **S$89**. Please add **S$43** if air mail delivery is required.

74

ORDER FORM

Manager	Name & Address of Purchaser
Europhone Language Institute #04-33 Peninsula Shopping Centre 3 Coleman Street Singapore 179804	Address _____ _____ _____

Dear Sir

We wish to order the books/book-cassettes* listed below and enclose a

international Money Order/ Bankdraft for S$ _____

----

*Delete as appropriate   Signature & Date

	State the Chosen Language in the Column below.			
Item	Simple / Basic * Book-Cassette	Unit Cost S$	Quantity	Total Cost S$

Payment to be made in Singapore dollars.   S$___ _____

Remarks_____

Notes

Simple Book-Cassettes are described in the inner front cover and cost **S$79** including surface mail. Please add **S$26** if air mail delivery is required.

Basic Book-Cassettes are described in the inner back cover and cost **S$89** including surface mail. Please add **S$43** if air mail delivery is required.

TOWARDS A BETTER HOLIDAY

House of Parliament in Kuala Lumpur.

Millions have begun to leave home to explore the world they came to know through television, radio and books. Airports can no longer hold them and airlines are bidding for bigger and faster aircraft. New opportunities abound for businessmen and travellers to explore the world.

At Europhone Institute our aim has been to constantly upgrade our publications and educational products to give better value to our patrons. Following the addition of dictionaries to all our language teaching books, the creation of this section on travel information is our latest innovation.

We hope this section will equip travellers to avoid the pitfalls peculiar to each country. Hopefully they will be sensitive to the way of life in the host country and harmonise with the people and their culture. A better holiday and more favourable responses from the people they meet will be their reward — a step towards better international understanding and goodwill.   *Have a Good Holiday!*

Publishers

TRAVEL GUIDE TO MALAYSIA

FOCUS ON KUALA LUMPUR

by

K.P. Sivam, MBA, MCIM, GDMM

DISCLAIMER

Every effort has been made by the publisher and authors to ensure that the Travel Guide is up-to-date. However, the publisher does not take responsibility for the information in it. Facilities, situations and circumstances are constantly changing resulting in some information becoming inaccurate by the time you get there. Please write and advise us of changes you notice. Thank you.

MAP OF KUALA LUMPUR

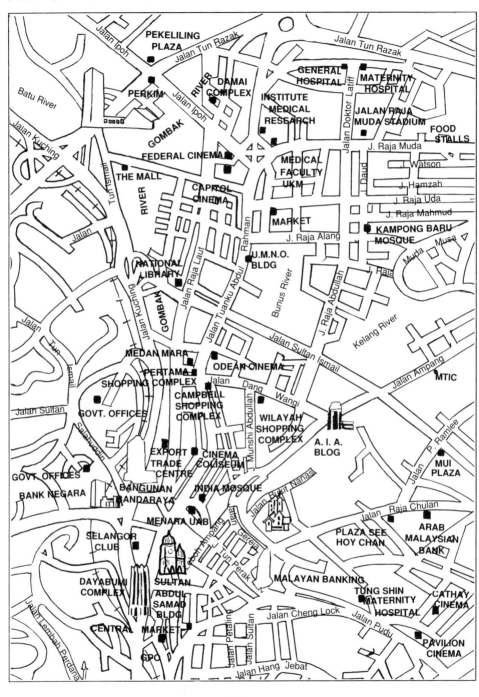

CONTENTS

1

MALAYSIA - A Brief History

Flagship of Albuquerque

At an early stage of human civilization, the Malay peninsula bridged continental Asia to the lands of the southwest Pacific. Prehistoric men took this route to their present homes in Indonesia, Malanesia and Australia. At the time of the Roman empire and the beginning of Christianity, there was trading between settlements in Kedah, Johore and Borneo. Trade with China and India had also commenced. The first Malay kingdom was in Kedah as a part of the Buddhist kingdom of Langkasuka that traded with India and Cambodia. In the 9th century, another Buddhist-Malay kingdom in Palembang, (Sumatra) called Sri Vijaya conquered Langkasuka, Kelantan, Trengganu and Pahang and became the dominant power in the Malay peninsula. In the 13th century colonists from this empire settled in Temasek (Singapore) to form a separate kingdom.

Malacca

Stadthuys (Town Hall) in Malacca.

Its Emergence

At the beginning of the 14th century, a powerful Hindu-Javanese empire called Majapahit arose in Java. It overthrew the Sri Vijaya empire and took Temasek, parts of the Malay peninsula, Borneo and east Sumatra. Prince Parameswara had left his native Palembang to settle in Temasek but had to move to Malacca in 1403 when Majapahit forces destroyed Temasek. Malacca's development drew Arab, Indian, Chinese and European trading ships. In 1406 Parameswara received recognition from the Ming Emperor of China who offered to protect him from the Thais, whose presence in Temasek was a constant threat. This help was gladly accepted and trade grew between the countries. In 1414 the prince became a Muslim and paved the way for Arab teachers and traders to promote

Islam and trade. Malacca prospered as commerce grew with China, the Islamic world and India.

The European Powers

In 1511 the Portuguese under the naval commander, Alfonso d' Albuqueque laid seige to Malacca and took it from the Malays. Their rule lasted 130 years, until 1641 when the Dutch ousted them to ensure that Malacca would not rival their Batavia (Jakarta) in commercial importance. Their occupation ended 174 years later in 1815 when the British took it in exchange for Bencoolen in Sumatra.

Early Malay States

The Dutch had to contend with the Riau-Johore Malay state which had a strong influence in the Malay peninsula. Kedah, Kelantan and Trengganu came under intermittent Thai control. From 1743 Selangor was under Bugis sultans and by 1773 Sumatran influence prevailed in the Minangkabau states of Negri Sembilan. The presence of the colonial powers for 446 years caused the decline of Malay political power. The Riau royal family split into Dutch and British branches. Pahang and Johore became sultanates. In the 17th century Brunei's control over Borneo was reduced when the Dutch set up trading posts along its coast. By the 19th century the sultan only controlled Sarawak and North Borneo (Sabah).

Second World War

Early in the second world war (1939–1945), the Japanese drove out the British and took over Malaya and Borneo. When the Allied Forces defeated Japan; the control of these states reverted to the British.

Malaysia

British sovereignty ceased in 1957 after 142 years when the Federation of Malaya was given independence. The larger Malaysia was formed in 1963 when the Malay peninsula, Sabah, Sarawak and Singapore merged into one country. Singapore separated from the fold in 1965.

MALAYSIA TODAY

The new and the old in Kuala Lumpur.

Location

Malaysia has an area of about 330,434 sq km (127,316 sq mi) covering the Malay Peninsular (West Malaysia) and the states of Sabah and Sarawak (East Malaysia). The two regions lie 531 km apart in the South China Sea. Peninsular Malaysia is 131,587 sq km while Sarawak and Sabah are 201,083 sq km. The country is situated just north of the equator in Southeast Asia. To its south are Singapore and Indonesia, to the north, Thailand and to the east, the Philippines. The natural vegetation is tropical rain forest. Human effort has converted over 4 million acres into rubber, palm oil plantations etc.

Sunny Days

Being near the equator the average annual temperature is between 21°C and 32°C. The climate is influenced by the

2

South-west and North-east monsoons.The days are nearly always sunny and warm and the humidity averages 87%. The nights are cool. The annual rainfall is from 2000 cm to 2500 cm. While it can rain at any time, generally showers are in the afternoons. The wet season is from November to February and affects the East Coast of Peninsula Malaysia, Sabah and Sarawak. The West Coast of Peninsula Malaysia is wet in the months of August and September.

The Racial Make-up

Malaysia has a population of about 16.2 million with West Malaysia having 13.4 million people and East Malaysia the rest of the 2.8 million inhabitants.Three major races make up Malaysia: the Malays (56.5%), the Chinese (32.8%) and the Indians (10.1%). Sabah and Sarawak comprise East Malaysia. The former has 84.2%. Malays and 14.9% Chinese whereas the latter has a population of 70.1% Malays and 28.7% Chinese. The population is young - 38.3% being below 15 years of age.

Religion

There is religious toleration in the country. Islam, Buddhism, Taoism, Hinduism and Christianity are practised by their adherents without interference from the state. The official religion is Islam which is the religion of the Malays.

Time

The time is eight hours ahead of G.M.T. and 16 hours ahead of the U.S. Pacific Standard Time.

Fauna

In the forests live a great variety of animals, including the elephant, rhino and the *seladang* (wild ox), the *orang utan* (of the ape family), tiger, panther, leopard, mousedeer, wild boar and monkey. Over 500 species of birds, many migratory, share the forests. The colourful ones include the kingfisher, sunbird, broadbills, golden aurioles and pittas.

A garden city that is Kuala Lumpur.

Education

A common curriculum and syllabus are used in all the schools to develop students with a common outlook and identity. Malay is the medium of instruction and English is a compulsory second language. Educational levels are categorised as primary, lower secondary, higher secondary and pre-university. There are seven universities and numerous colleges, institutes, polytechnics and vocational schools.

The Administration

Malaysia is made up of 13 states of which nine have hereditary rulers. The King (Yang di-Pertuan Agong) is the Supreme Head of State. He is elected from among the nine rulers and his tenure of service is for five years. The Prime Minister, is the head of the government. Parliament comprises two Houses: All of the Dewan Rakyat (Lower House of Representatives) are members elected by the electorate to serve for five years. The Dewan Negara (Senate) has members who have been nominated by the King to assist for six years. They are chosen for their distinguished public service. Some are outstanding professionals and leaders of racial minorities. The Prime Minister heads the Cabinet of ministers. A Chief Minister or Menteri Besar is elected to serve each of the 13 states which have their own elected State Assembly.

Free Enterprise

The cornerstone of the economy is free enterprise. Malaysia has an economy based on primary products but is rapidly industrialising. To expedite industrial development a number of government agencies have been set up.They include the Malaysian Industrial Development Authority (MIDA) and the Heavy Industries Corporation (HICOM). The country is one of the world's largest producers of palm oil, tin and rubber. Other important products include petroleum, timber and pepper. A high yielding industry is transportation. Air services are an essential component and Malaysian Airlines System (MAS) is a major contributor to the industry. Tourism offers great promise as a foreign exchange earner. Four million tourists are expected this year and there are positive signs of steady growth in the years ahead.

Foreign Relations

Malaysia has 67 diplomatic missions in 57 countries that include the U.S., the U.K., the U.S.S.R., China and the major European countries. Accreditations exist with a further 34 countries. Through this network of offices, Malaysia promotes cordial relations with all friendly nations in the international community. There are 77 countries which have missions accredited to Malaysia. United Nations representation in Malaysia is through the following agencies which have offices in Kuala Lumpur: UNICEF, UNHCR, WHO, FAO. Malaysia has played an active role in bringing peace and prosperity to the region and the world. It works through ASEAN, the OIC, the Non-Aligned Movement and the UN.

Flora

The warm tropical climate and the dense rain forests which cover 70% of Malaysia provide an ideal habitat for thousands of plants, insects, birds and animals. Parts of the forests are believed to have been untampered with for millions of years. Over 15,000 species of plants have been identified and recorded and of these over 6,000 are trees from which timber is gathered. The popular types of timber are Changal, Keruing, Meranti, Jelutong, Balam and Merbau. Creepers (Lianes), orchids, ferns and aroids are plentiful.

The Constitution

The supreme law of the country is the Constitution of Malaysia. It lays down the rights and obligations of the individual and states the limits and circumstances under which they may be varied. It protects citizens from retrospective criminal laws and repeated trials. It ensures freedom of speech and assembly; it guarantees freedom of worship and the right to own property. The Constitution may be altered by Parliament only if two-thirds of its members support the amendment.

The Conference of Rulers

The Conference exists by the authority of the Constitution. It consists of the Rulers of the states and elects the Yang di Pertuan Agong and his deputy. It must be consulted for the appointment of judges, the Attorney-General, the Elections Commission and the Public Services Commission. Its powers extend to all matters affecting the rights of the Malays, the natives of Sabah and Sarawak and those of the Rulers themselves.

3

PLANNING THE TRIP

Tourist Information Centre at Railway Station, KL.

Climate

Malaysia is sunny, hot and humid throughout the year except for the months of April, May and October when the west coast of Peninsula Malaysia receives rain. During the months of November to February it rains in the east coast of Peninsula Malaysia and the north eastern part of Sabah. When planning your trip you should take into account the wet months to get the best out of your holiday.

Customs Formalities

Customs duty is waived on personal effects so long as the quantities are reasonable. The following duty free goods may be imported by each foreigner: 200 cigarettes or 225 grams of tobacco; wines, spirits or any other liquor up to one litre; cosmetics, soap and dentifrices up to M$200 in value, 100 sticks of matches, apparel not exceeding three pieces, not more than one pair of footwear and one unit each of a portable electrical appliance for personal care and hygiene.

Health Regulations

Innoculations for smallpox and cholera are not required for travellers entering Malaysia. A vaccination is only necessary for arrival from infected areas and from yellow fever endemic zones. These requirements do not apply to children who are under one year of age.

Advance Bookings

For pleasant travel and visits to hill and beach resorts, it is advisable to make bookings at least one month before the peak periods mentioned below. During such times, public transport may be difficult to get and hotel accommodation will be scarce. Christmas and New Year – 24th December to 3rd of January; Chinese New Year – in January or February, Hari Raya Puasa – in April or May.

Immigration

Foreign visitors must be in possession of a valid passport or other internationally recognised travel document endorsed for entry into Malaysia. Travel documents are also necessary for a visit to the East Malaysian states of Sabah and Sarawak.

Currency

The Ringgit (Dollar, M$1), the local currency, is equivalent to US$0.4. Coins and notes of various denominations are available. Malaysian currency may be purchased at banks, major hotels and airports.

Airport Tax

Airport tax for visitors departing to Singapore is 5 Ringgit. Visitors leaving for other destinations in the world, pay an airport tax of 15 Ringgit.

3

Heading for the City

Many of the tourists arriving in Kuala Lumpur use taxis or buses to get to the city. To use a taxi, a voucher has to be purchased at an airport counter. The rates are fixed according to one's destination. It costs about 16 Ringgit to travel from the airport to the city. Buses leave for the city at intervals of 30 minutes and charge $1.20 per trip. There is a bus stop just outside the main airport building.

Time

Malaysian time is eight hours ahead of G.M.T. and 16 hours ahead of U.S. Pacific Standard Time. Both Malaysia and Singapore observe the same time.

Dangerous Drugs

The import of heroin, cocaine and other dangerous drugs is prohibited. Trafficking in them, even in small quantities, is a serious offence and carries the death penalty.

Motoring

The importation of a motor vehicle is permitted without fees, provided it is re-exported within 90 days. Entry points in the north are at the Thai border towns of Padang Besar, Changloon and Kroh. In the south, it is at Johore Bahru which is about 20 km from Singapore. Ports of entry are Port Klang and Penang. Insurance against Third Party Risks is compulsory. Driving is on the left-hand side of the road and an International Driving Licence is necessary.

Malaysians enjoy sports and sporting events. Soccer is immensely popular among them. They are also fond of tennis, golf, squash and motor-racing. Gaining acceptance are windsurfing and sailing. Traditional pastimes include *sepak takraw* (a game played with a rattan ball between two teams), topspinning and kite-flying. Enthusiasm for jogging and walking is increasing daily. Each community in Malaysia has its own traditional dances. Malaysian artists and artistes are researching their cultures for new themes in dance, drama and in the arts.

MAKING THE MOST OF YOUR STAY

The Railway Station in Kuala Lumpur.

Mailing

Post offices operate from 8.00 am. to 5.00 pm. except on Saturdays when they open from 8.00 am. to 12.45 pm. Mailing services are available at most hotels and letters with stamps may be posted at any public mail box.

Public Telephones

Local calls cost 10 cents for three minutes. At public phones, remember to press the release button once the person you call responds. Phone cards may be purchased for 5 Ringgit or more at Petronas petrol pumps and shops near telephone booths.

International Calls

Please dial 108 for the International Telephone Exchange Operator. Overseas calls may be made from public tele-

4

phones at the Central Telegraph Office at the Kuala Lumpur International Airport between 7.30 am. and 11.30 pm.

Clothing

The climate is warm and the dry season is from March to November. It is humid but pleasant most of the time. The nights are cool. Wear light clothes and convenient shoes.

Office Hours

Governments offices operate between 8 am. and 4 pm. Banks open from 10 am. to 3 pm. Many business offices open at 9 am. and function till 5 pm.

Air and Rail Transport

The national carrier, Malaysia Airlines has a fleet serving 35 international destinations. The domestic service links Kuala Lumpur with Ipoh, Penang, Alor Setar, Langkawi, Kota Bharu, Kota Kinabalu, Sandakan, Lahad Datu, Tawau, Labuan, Kuching, Sibu, Bintulu and Miri. Within Peninsula Malaysia, Pelangi Air flies to Kuala Lumpur, Ipoh, Penang, Sitiawan, Alor Setar, Langkawi, Malacca, Taman Negara, Tioman Island, Kuantan, Kerteh and Kuala Terengganu.

Helicopter and private planes may be chartered. The railways connect Thailand and Singapore with the main towns of Peninsula Malaysia. Tickets for air-conditioned coaches during the day and first class or second class coaches at night with berths are available. First class cabins are for two males or two females. One may therefore have to share a cabin with a strange bedfellow. Advanced bookings of up to one week are recommended.

Flight Information

For a list of airlines, please refer to the Contents page.

Banks

There are more than 40 commercial banks with over 600 branches in the country. Banks open for 5½ days a week.

Banking hours are as follows: 10.00 am. to 3.00 pm. Monday to Friday; 10.00 am. to 11.30 am. on Saturday; Banks are closed on Sunday. Johore, Kedah, Perlis, Kelantan and Trengganu have their weekend on Thursday and Friday. Government offices close at 1 pm. on Thursday and banks operate from 10.00 am. to 11.30 am. All government offices are closed on Friday but banks open from 10.00 am. to 3.00 pm.

Tipping

Tipping is not compulsory. Hotel porters, waiters, taxi drivers and other service personnel will not demand a tip but will willingly accept one. Hotels and restaurants add a 10% charge for service. A 5% tax is payable to the government.

Taxis

Taxis are the most convenient means of travel and the rates are among the cheapest in the world. Taxis may be stopped as they cruise, although taxi stands may be found outside prominent buildings. The rates are $1.00 for the first 1.6 km and 30 cents for each subsequent 0.8 km for air-conditioned vehicles. Between 12 a.m. and 6 a.m. there is a 50% surcharge.

Flight Time

Flight time to Singapore from Kuala Lumpur is 45 minutes. Bangkok is two and a half hours away. It takes six hours to reach Tokyo and one and a half hours to reach Jakarta.

Languages

The official language is Bahasa Malaysia (Malay) which is the medium of instruction in schools and universities. English is a compulsory second language. Nearly everyone speaks it. The Indians who comprise about 10% of the population speak Tamil, Hindi and other Indian languages. The Chinese speak Mandarin and several dialects, notably Cantonese and Hokkien.

4

Bus Fares

Omnibus charges begin at 20 cents whereas the standard fare for minibuses is 50 cents. Buses to cities and towns in Peninsula Malaysia leave the Pudu Raya Bus Station in Kuala Lumpur. A guide to fares is given below. They may be increased without notice.

Towns	M$	Towns	M$
Alor Setar	19.50	Johore Baru	15.20
Butterworth	15.50	Kuantan	11.00
Ipoh	8.50	Kuala Trengganu	20.00
Malacca	8.00	Kota Baru	25.00

Train Services

Tickets for 1st and 2nd class seats may be purchased 30 days in advance. For reservations and fare information, please call Kuala Lumpur, 03-2747442 or 03-2747443.

Dial-a-Taxi

To get around in Kuala Lumpur you can dial a taxi:

	Tel
Federal Territory & S'gor Radio Taxi Ass.	2936211
KL Taxi Drivers' Association	2434472
Koteksi	2411022

Traveller's Cheques & Credit Cards

An unlimited amount of Traveller's Cheques may be brought into the country. Credit cards are also welcome. The better known ones are: American Express, Visa, Master, Diner's Club, Carte Blanche and Bank of America.

Medical Facilities

If you are in need of medical assistance, call the receptionist at your hotel. All towns and cities have government hospitals, (called *General Hospital*) where medical attention is free.

WHERE TO STAY IN KUALA LUMPUR

The Shangrila Hotel in Kuala Lumpur.

Western type hotels are found in all the major towns in Malaysia. There are luxury hotels, medium class hotels and budget priced hotels. A 10% service charge and 5% government tax are added to bills at tourist establishments. Tipping is done at the discretion of the guest. The following hotels in Kuala Lumpur offer much choice.

Best Hotels in the City	Telephone Numbers	Single Room Price Range
Shangrila Hotel	(03) 2322388	$200 – $300
Kuala Lumpur Hilton	(03) 2422222	$200 – $300
Pan Pacific Hotel	(03) 4425555	$200 – $300
Park Royal Hotel	(03) 2425588	$200 – $300
Ming Court Hotel	(03) 2618888	$200 – $300

5

Moderately Priced Hotels	Telephone Numbers	Single Room Price Range
Hotel Equatorial	(03) 2617777	$120 – $200
The Federal Hotel	(03) 2489166	$120 – $200
Holiday Inn City Centre	(03) 2939233	$120 – $200
Merlin Hotel	(03) 2420033	$120 – $200
Park Avenue Hotel	(03) 2428333	$120 – $200
Malaysia Hotel	(03) 2428033	$120 – $200

Less Expensive Hotels	Telephone Numbers	Single Room Price Range
Furama Hotel	(03) 2301777	$90 – $100
The Lodge	(03) 2420122	$90 – $100
Hotel Malaya	(03) 2327722	$70 – $80
Mandarin Hotel	(03) 2303000	$90 – $100
The Plaza Hotel	(03) 2982255	$90 – $120
South East Asia Hotel	(03) 2926077	$80 – $90
Sungai Wang Hotel	(03) 2485255	$80 – $90

Hotel rooms are also available for as little as 30 Ringgit. They provide the bare necessities and guests have to use a common bathroom.

Budget Priced Hotels

Cheap hotels can be found along Jalan Tuanku Abdul Rahman. 100 metres from the Odeon theatre in Jalan Tuanku Abdul Rahman is the Shiraz Hotel (Tel 03-2920159) which has rooms at M$40. At No 285 of the same road is the Dashrun Hotel, charging M$40 for singles and M$50 for doubles. The Nanyang Hotel at 83 Jalan Sultan in Chinatown charges M$30 for singles and M$40 for doubles. A cheap hotel in Jalan Sultan is the Lee Mun Hotel where a room costs only M$20. The Lido Hotel on Jalan Thambapillai in Brickfields has rooms at M$30 to M$35. The Hotel Pudu Raya (Tel 03-2321000) is 15 storeys high and is above the Pudu Raya bus station. Rooms cost between M$50 to M$55.

Youth Hostels, YWCA, YMCA

There are numerous youth hostels which are listed in the Telephone Directory. There is also a YWCA and YMCA in Kuala Lumpur. The former is in Jalan Hang Jebat, Tel 03-2383225, while the latter is at Jalan Padang Belia, Tel 03-2741439. One youth hostel is Wisma Belia (MAYC), Tel 03-2744833. Book your rooms early.

Hotels Close to Airport	Tel Numbers	Room Rental
1 **Petaling Jaya Hilton** 2, Jalan Barat 46200 Petaling Jaya	03-7559122	From M$190
2 **Hyatt Saujana** Subang International Airport Highway, 46710 Petaling Jaya	03-7461188	From M$180
3 **Subang Airport Hotel** Subang International Airport 47200 Subang	03-7462122	From M$130
4 **The Merlin Subang** Subang Jaya, 47509 Petaling Jaya	03-7335211	From M$170
5 **Shah's Village Motel** 3 & 5, Lorong Sultan 46710 Petaling Jaya	03-7569702	From M$95
6 **South Pacific Hotel** 7, Jalan 52/16 46200 Petaling Jaya	03-7569922	From M$29

Petaling Jaya is midway between the airport and the city.

6

WHAT TO SEE IN KUALA LUMPUR & MALAYSIA

The Central Market.

Kuala Lumpur was founded in 1875 and became the capital of the new Federated Malay States in 1896. It gained city status in 1972 while it was the capital of Selangor. 1974 saw its elevation to Federal capital with a Mayor as the head of the city. With a cosmopolitan population of 1.2 million it is 243 square km in area. Many places of interest in the city have been identified below.

The Central Market

Built by the British in 1928 it is situated in the heart of the city. It was a wet market that has been converted into a commercial and recreational hub. Some compare it to Covent Gardens in London and others to Fisherman's Wharf in San Francisco. Modernised, it houses all kinds of traditional goods such as basketry, silverware, batik paintings, drift-wood, pottery and pewterware. Handicraft can be made to order and you can have your portrait painted in an hour at a reasonable price. Budding musicians, artistes and handicraft experts display their skills. There are 10 restaurants and over 200 specialised shops.

Karyaneka Handicraft Village

A beautiful cluster of buildings in traditional Malay architecture is located at Jalan Raja Chulan. This village displays beautiful handicrafts from all 13 states of Malaysia. It comprises an aviary, a fish pond, the National Crafts Museum and an Ethno-Botanic Garden. It is an ideal stop for souvenir hunters and is open daily from 9.00 am. to 6.00 pm.

China Town

The bustling activity which is in Jalan Petaling is best enjoyed at night when fluorescent lights enhance the ambiance. Lighted up are a multitude of open air restaurants and stalls selling clothing, electronic goods, toys and all manner of household goods. You can feast on authentic Chinese food, local fruit and confectionery.

National Art Gallery

The gallery which is located in Jalan Sultan Hishamuddin, occupies the premises of the former Majestic Hotel, once popular with British expatriates. It displays a beautiful collection of the works of local artists. The gallery opens daily from 10 am. to 6 pm. except on Fridays when it opens from 12 noon to 3 pm. Admission is free.

A Hindu Temple in Chinatown

A double treat awaits the visitor to Chinatown where a Hindu temple stands incongruously alongside Chinese shops. Built in 1873 and called the Sri Maha-Mariaman Temple, it is one of the largest and most ornate of temples. It is decorated with gold ornaments, intricate carvings of Hindu deities, and exquisite Spanish tiles. Leave your shoes outside the temple and wander respectfully around the temple. Visit it by 5.00 pm. and you may hear bells and chanting as priests conduct *pujas* – prayers in supplication of assistance on behalf of worshippers.

6

The National Museum

The National Museum.

Located along Jalan Damansara, of Sumatran (Minangkabau) architecture is the museum with a fine collection of historical artifacts and specimens of the fauna of Malaysia. The displays include arts and crafts, weapons, currency, birds, animals and insects.

Istana Negara

This is the official residence of His Majesty, The Yang Di Pertuan Agong, Malaysia's King and Supreme Head of State. Situated along Jalan Istana, the palace is surrounded by well maintained green lawns. The palace is often transformed into a fairyland of multicoloured lights, arches and decorations to celebrate national events.

The Sultan Abdul Samad Building

The outstanding feature of this building is its historical clock tower. Built between 1894-97 are its curving arches and domes, the highest of which measures 41 metres. It is an attraction much adored by visitors. The building houses the offices and courts of the Malaysian Judiciary and provides a distinct character to the city.

The Merdeka Square (Dataran Merdeka)

Originally the Royal Selangor Club field (padang), it is in front of the Sultan Abdul Samad Building. Public occassions like the National Day on 31st August are celebrated here. It is a historical landmark and public attraction. Of pride to the country is the newly erected flag pole which at 100 metres is believed to be the tallest in the world. A unique underground shopping centre and car park exists.

The Lake Gardens

The Parliament buildings in Jalan Parlimen are surrounded by beautiful landscaped gardens, a picturesque lake, an orchid garden, a butterfly farm and a deer park. The lake has facilities for boating and the orchid garden has more than 800 species of orchids. During weekends and public holidays the garden is converted into an orchid bazaar. This is the Lake Garden.

Malaysia Tourist Information Centre

Built in 1935 along Jalan Ampang is a building that was the headquarters of the British Army in 1941. It was the Japanese Imperial Army Headquarters after Japan invaded Malaysia. Now it is a tourist office that provides information on the 13 states of Malaysia and houses an exhibition hall, an auditorium, a souvenir shop, a restaurant and a travel service counter. Cultural performances are often staged here.

6

National Monument

It is a bronze monument that depicts the victory of the Malaysian Security Forces over the communists. The memorial honours the Malaysian and Commonwealth forces who fought the enemy in the 1950s.

Lake Titiwangsa

Minutes away from the city and situated between Jalan Pahang and Jalan Tun Razak is Lake Titiwangsa. This re-creational park has a man-made lake and green landscaped surroundings. It is a haven for joggers and nature lovers. Pony rides, canoeing, aquabiking, tennis and squash are popular activities here.

Batu Caves

North of the Federal Territory of Kuala Lumpur are caves with shrines of the Hindu diety, Lord Muruga, also known as Lord Subramaniam. During the festival of Thaipusam, in the month of February over a hundred thousand devotees visit the caves to pay homage and fulfil vows. They pierce their bodies with spikes, hooks and small spears and walk up the 274 steps to shrines at the top of the cliffs. You can take minibus No 11 at Jalan Pudu to get there.

Mimaland

Mimaland is a sprawling recreational resort of 320 hectares of secondary jungle. It offers facilities for swimming, fishing, boating and jungle trekking. Chalets at the edge of the lake are available but booking in advance is always necessary.

Two Gardens in One

ASEAN is the acronym for the Association of South East Asian nations. It comprises Malaysia, Singapore, Indonesia, Philippines, Thailand and Brunei Darussalam. The ASEAN Garden is an attractively landscaped garden that displays the sculptures of the best artists in ASEAN.

NATIONAL ATTRACTIONS IN MALAYSIA

Ferry leaving for Penang (in background)

Pulau Langkawi

Langkawi which is part of the State of Kedah is a group of 104 islands, most of which are uninhabited. It is for those who are looking for the ultimate in tropical island beauty. Legends abound in the islands of forsaken maidens and forelorn princes. They shroud Langkawi with a romantic and mystical aura. Swimming, fishing, scuba diving, boating, golf, tennis and pony trekking are popular pastimes. A duty-free shop makes available liquor, tobacco, perfumes and electronic appliances at bargain prices.

Pulau Tioman

A paradise unspoilt by modern civilization, this island lies off the coast of Pahang. It is 39 km long and 19 km wide. It takes 3 hours by launch from the town of Mersing on the mainland to get to Tioman. If you are flying from Kuala Lumpur or Singapore you may take direct flights for a pleasant and quick entry into the island. Tioman is a rare treat with clear waters that enable you to see coral and the beautiful inhabitants of the underworld. The reefs and crystal clear sea make it ideal for snorkelling and photography. Bird watching is another favourite activity. Tioman waits to be explored.

Cameron Highlands

Cameron Highlands which is about 4,500 feet above sea level was founded in 1885 by William Cameron. It is a popular hill resort because of its cool climate and lush vegetation. Agricultural products and tea are its exports. Conducted tours to its beautiful rose gardens are a daily event and for sportsmen there is an 18-hole golf course. Accommodation is available at the Merlin Hotel, Ye Old Smoke House, Strawberry Park Hotel and the Golf Course Inn.

Genting Highlands

This Highland is a well developed hill resort. It is situated 1,524 metres above sea level and is only 80 km from Kuala Lumpur. Regular temperatures drop to 15°C amidst blue skies and brilliant sunshine. Its star attraction is a first class casino. Fortune seekers come from as far as Singapore, Indonesia and Thailand. A four star hotel, a theatre restaurant, a 16-lane bowling alley, a lake, an 18-hole golf course and an amusement centre are facilities for non-gamblers.

Taman Negara

A park for the preservation of wildlife and plants is Taman Negara (National Park). Situated in 4,343 square km of dense forest, it is for hikers and mountain climbers. The Gunung Tahan range with a peak at 2,190 metres high may be reached on foot in two days. Trekkers are advised to use local guides and to take sufficient food, water and camping equipment. The adventure is not for the faint hearted.

Penang

Penang island off the north-western coast of Peninsula Malaysia, like Malacca is steeped in history. Its other part, Province Wellesley, is on the mainland. Founded in 1786 by Francis Light as a British trading outpost, it is today a bustling city with a blend of cultures from the East and West. Its beaches, the Penang Hill, the Snake Temple, Fort Cornwallis and the Penang Bird Park are tourist attractions.

Sepilok Orang Utan Sanctuary (Sabah)

This sanctuary is in Sandakan, a town in the state of Sabah. It is a forest reserve of 4,440 hectares of equatorial rain forest with a wealth of rare plants, animals and birds. The sanctuary cares for orang utans which have strayed into logging camps or who have hurt themselves. They are released into the forest when they recover from their injuries.

Niah National Park (Miri)

The park is deep in the jungles of Miri. It can be reached by flying, road and boat. From Kuching visitors may fly to Miri and then travel by road to Batu Niah to hire a boat to the park. The Niah National Park covers 3,103 hectares of forest and limestone caves. It extends over 11 hectares and is a source of edible bird's nests which are collected from the ceiling of the caves. Bird's nest soup is a Chinese delicacy.

Sarawak

In 1839 James Brooke, an English adventurer came to Sarawak when there was rebellion against the Sultan of Brunei. He promptly quelled the unrest and in 1841 was made the Rajah of Sarawak by the ruler, Pengiran Mahkota of Brunei. James was succeeded in 1868 by Charles Brooke and in 1917 by Charles Vyner. Sarawak and Sabah were taken by the Japanese in 1942 but were reoccupied by the British in 1945 after the second world war. In 1963 the two states joined Malaysia. Sarawak is the largest state in Malaysia and is about 124,000 sq. km. The economic and political centre of the state is Kuching with a population of 306,000 people. It was declared a city in 1988 and its largest town is Miri. With an economy based on natural gas, timber, pepper, palm oil, rubber, cocoa and urea, its future is very bright.

Sabah

In 1881 the British North Borneo Company began to administer Sabah, then known as British North Borneo. Sabah was granted freedom by the British to join Malaysia in 1963. It is the second largest state in Malaysia and is 1900 km. from Kuala Lumpur. Singapore is 1600 km. away.

Malacca

Malacca's best known history dates back to the 13th century. After its founding by the Indonesian Hindu prince, Parameswara (Raja Iskandar Shah, when he became a Muslim), there followed a continuous period of colonial rule – the Portuguese from 1511, the Dutch from 1641 and the British from 1824 up to 1957. This varied European influence has left Malacca one of the richest legacies anywhere of relics for tourists, archeologists and historians.

Places to Visit

Bukit China (Chinese Hill) is the enclave created in the 15th century by the Sultan of Malacca for his beautiful bride, the princess from the Ming Empire of China. Over 160 acres are preserved, part of it as the burial ground of famous Chinese. *St. Paul's Church*, built in 1521 by the Portuguese, was used by St. Francis Xavier. *Porta de Santiago* is the Portuguese fortress which survives despite British efforts to demolish it in 1807. The oldest Dutch building in the East is the *Stadthuys* (Town Hall), now serving as a government office. It is a fine specimen of Dutch masonry and woodwork. Another Dutch monument is *Christ Church* that was built in 1753 of pink bricks imported from the Netherlands. It is a tribute to Dutch architecture and is today an Anglican church. It has louvre windows and ceiling beams of 48 feet in length. A lustrous painting of *The Last Supper* adorns the church. A collection of silver vessels are on view and bear the Dutch coat-of-arms. *The Tranquerah Mosque*, was built over 150 years ago. Within it is the tomb of the Sultan of Johore who ceded Singapore to the British.

Antiques

Shops in Jalan Hang Jebat are well-known to antique collectors all over the world. Artifacts from as far back as the 17th century can be purchased here at reasonable prices.

Portuguese Square

Situated at the Portuguese Settlement is the Square, a complex of structures manifesting Portuguese architecture. It is more an entertainment centre. Portuguese food is available and at night the cafes cater for tourists in search of light entertainment. Bands play old Portuguese melodies and visitors are treated to song and dance events.

Cheng Hoon Teng Temple

Founded in 1646, this is the oldest Chinese temple in Malaysia. Materials for the building were brought from China. Mythological figures of porcelain and glass decorate its eaves. Symbols of Buddhism, Confucianism and Taoism are on display in different sections of the temple. St. John's Fort, a former Portuguese chapel was rebuilt by the Dutch in the 18th century. It stands on St. John's Hill and is 3 km from Malacca town.

8

WHERE TO EAT AND DRINK IN KUALA LUMPUR

Jalan Leboh Ampang's Indian restaurants

Variety of food

Food may be had at all times and at reasonable prices. A satisfying meal could cost as little as three to five Ringgit. As many races live in Malaysia a great variety of food is available, in posh restaurants, at open air stalls and coffee shops.

Open Air Restaurants

Having a meal in the open air, seated on wooden stools with matching cowboy type collapsable round tables is a characteristic Malaysian experience. Some excellent food is sold under make-shift canopies or trees. A well known fish-head curry food centre is in Sentul, just off the main road and is opposite a defunct cinema. The crowd for lunch includes executives and big wigs who come in their limousines. Similar clusters of stalls that come alive at night are at Jalan Brickfields, Jalan Bukit Bintang, Jalan Imbi and Jalan Kampong Baru. One such place operates on the top floor of the Central Market. Patrons desiring greater comfort will find the coffee-houses in their hotels a good place to eat. Some hotel restaurants, like the Hilton, Merlin and Equatorial, stage cultural shows. Familiarise yourself with the following dishes before visiting the restaurants.

Satay

Satay is meat that is marinated in spices, skewered through a stick and barbequed over a charcoal stove. It is eaten with a peanut sauce and *ketupat* (cooked rice in a little bag of woven coconut leaves).

Murtabak

Wheat dough is used in this pancake like bread. Minced meat marinated with spices, eggs, onions and chillies are placed on the rolled out dough which is then folded up and cooked on an oiled griddle. It is served with pickled onions and curry.

Nasi Lemak

Nasi Lemak is rice cooked in coconut milk. It is served with anchovies, sliced boiled eggs, fried peanuts and cucumber. Wrapped in banana leaf, it is a popular snack. Elaborate versions are served with curries.

Thosai

Thosai is made from a liquid mixture of rice and lentil flour. The mixture is poured onto a griddle and when cooked looks like a pancake. Eaten with coconut *chutney* or curry, it is available in most Indian restaurants.

Tandori

Tandori is a North Indian speciality of skewered marinated chicken, beef, or fish baked in an upright dry earthenware

8

pot called the *tandoor*. The meal is eaten with *naan* (a bread of wheat flour).

Otak-otak

Lovers of *Nyonya* (of Malay and Chinese parentage) cuisine relish *otak-otak*. Minced fish mixed with spices is wrapped in coconut or banana leaf. The packing is roasted over an open fire.

Malay Food

Satay lovers patronise the following two comfortable restaurants which have a chain of restaurants in Malaysia and Singapore.

Satay Anika
Bukit Bintang Plaza, Jalan Bukit Bintang, Tel 03-2483113

Sate Ria
9 Jalan Tuanku Abdul Rahman, Tel 03-2911648

For Malay rice and curry to titillate the palate visit:

Bunga Raya Restaurant
Level 2 Putra World Trade Centre, Tel 03-2933888

Nelayan Floating Restaurant
Titiwangsa Lake Gardens, Tel 03-4228600

Chinese Food

Original Chinese cuisine comparable to the best in Hong Kong may be sampled in the better establishments. Venture into:

The Village Restaurant
320 Jalan Tun Razak, Tel 03-2418750

Mak Yee Restaurant
32 Jalan Sultan Ismail, Tel 03-2488060

Thai Food

A different oriental flavour may be savoured at Thai restaurants. Menus in English are available.

Restaurant Seri Chiangmei
14 Jalan Perak, Tel 03-2482927

Chilli Padi Thai Restaurant
2nd Floor, The Mall, Jalan Putra

Drinking Out

Coffee shops and road-side stalls may serve a glass of beer for 1.5 Ringgit. In a posh hotel bar, you have to pay five times as much. A well known watering hole is the Royal Selangor Club which is open only to members and their guests. Please refer to the *Contents* page for a longer list of restaurants and bars.

Entertainment

If you are looking for cultural entertainment, the Central Market is the place. Small international shows are staged at luxury hotels. If you enjoy music and dancing you can visit numerous discotheques in the city. The following places of entertainment are for your choice.

Nightclubs

Campbell Nightclub, 6th Floor, Campbell Complex. Tel 03-2929655. Grosder Nightclub, Bowling Alley Basement, Federal Hotel. Tel 03-2418002.

Japanese Lounges

Club Fukiko, 2nd Floor, Menara Promet, Jalan Sultan Ismail. Tel 03-2417489. Tapagayo, 2, Bintang Village, Jalan Bukit Bintang. Tel 03-2419029.

Discotheques

Limelight, 3, Changkat Raja Chulan. Tel 03-2387029. Stargazer, Penthouse, Semua House. Tel 03-2931597.

9

WHERE TO SHOP IN KUALA LUMPUR

Heading for Jalan Tuanku Abdul Rahman.

With its varied culture and access to Western markets, Kuala Lumpur offers much to the discriminating shopper. There is an abundance of handicraft — woodcarvings, silvercraft, batik printings, songket weaving, basketry and pottery. Most of the goods are sold in the many shopping centres that await your patronage. Visiting a *pasar malam* (night market) is a rare treat. The visitor can test his skills at bargaining and obtain good value for his money. One of these markets opens nightly in Chinatown at Jalan Petaling. At Jalan Tuanku Abdul Rahman another night market opens on Saturdays and is dominated by Malay vendors. Products such as paintings, batik, watches, clothes, fruit, leather goods, food and drinks are on sale. It is interesting to walk through this market. There are many large shopping centres which are air-conditioned. The newest of them are The

Mall and Lot 10 which cater for the well heeled. Price tags are used by some shops where prices are fixed. Credit cards are accepted in most of them. The popular shopping areas are along Jalan Bukit Bintang, Jalan Tuanku Abdul Rahman and Jalan Ampang.

	Names of Shopping Centres	Locations	Telephone
1	Ampang Park Shopping Complex	Jalan Ampang	03-2617006
2	Bukit Bintang Plaza	Jalan Bukit Bintang	03-2983937
3	Campbell Shopping Complex	Jalan Campbell	03-2922825
4	Central Market	Jalan Hang Kasturi	03-2749966
5	City Square	Jalan Tun Razak	03-2614970/5
6	Dayabumi Complex	Jal Sultan Hishamuddin	03-9855545
7	Globe Silk Store	Jal Tuanku Abdul Rahman	03-2922188
8	Hankyu Jaya	Jal Tuanku Abdul Rahman	03-4424866
9	Infokraf Malaysia	Jal Sultan Hishamuddin	03-2934929
10	Karyaneka	Jalan Raja Chulan	03-2431686
11	Kuala Lumpur Plaza	Jalan Bukit Bintang	03-2417288
12	Kota Raya Complex	Jalan Cheng Lock	03-2322564
13	Pertama Shopping Complex	Jalan Dang Wangi	03-2982533
14	The Weld	Jalan Raja Chulan	03-2610305
15	Yow Chuan Plaza	Jalan Ampang	03-2489400

Globe Silk Store

Shoppers desiring variety and reasonable prices may wish to visit Globe Silk Store at 185 Jalan Tuanku Abdul Rahman. This 10 storey department store was built in 1980 and serves as a one-stop emporium.

Selangor Pewter

The largest pewter factory in the world is Selangor Pewter at No 4 Jalan Usahawan Enam, Setapak. Its beautifully crafted ornaments are much sought after. The company uses methods of manufacture which have been handed down from generation to generation resulting in fine craftmanship. More than 700 different articles are produced and include flower vases, ash trays, memorial plaques, clocks, fruit bowls, trays, tankards and goblets. One of their showrooms is at Jalan Tuanku Abdul Rahman, next to the Odeon Theatre.

10

IF YOU NEED HELP

Merdeka Square, a stop for tourists.

For your well being read the following information.

Hospitals	Telephone
Assunta Hospital	7923433
Pantai Medical Centre	7575077
Subang Jaya Medical Centre	7341212
Tawakal Pusat Pakar	4237899
General Hospital (Government)	2921044
University Hospital	7564422
Tung Shin Hospital	2388900
Pudu Specialist Centre	2481146

Emergency Calls

Dial 999 for the Police, ambulance or the fire brigade.

Domestic Transportation

Travelling is possible by bus, taxi, rail and air. For a list of airlines, please refer to the *Contents* page.

Companies	Telephone
1 Malaysia Airlines System (National Carrier)	7463000
2 DCA Information (Civil Aviation)	7461235
3 Pelangi Air (Domestic flights)	7463000
4 Malaysian Railways	2747435
5 Mayflower Acme Tours Sdn. Bhd. (Car Rentals)	6276011
6 Pudu Raya Bus Station (Buses to other towns)	2388148

Service and Information

Telephone numbers may be dialled by day or night for assistance and information. Services include cars for hire, watch repairs, laundry, dancing lessons and secretarial assistance. Restaurants and day care centres may also be reached. The telephone numbers are *2300300* and *8009090*.

Tourist Police

You may seek the assistance of the Tourist Police.

Kuala Lumpur	03-2415522/243	Penang	04-375522
Malacca	06-222222	Kota Bahru	09-785534

Tourist Information

Centres providing information are as follows:

Kuala Lumpur	03-4411295, 2434929/91
Penang	04-619067/62
Kota Kinabalu	088-211698/732
Johore Bahru	07-223590/91
Kuching	082-246575/775

Visit Malaysia Year Hotline

Dial 800-90-90 toll-free from any part of Malaysia for instant information and assistance. The service is manned round-the-clock to ensure your pleasant stay in Malaysia. It is aided by computers with an IBM installed database. Information includes flight schedules.

10

Booking Your Tour

Most hotels have travel brochures and act as agents for tour organisations. You can make your bookings through them or directly with the organisations. Please refer to the *Contents* page for a list of travel agencies.

Bus Services

There are two types – the ordinary service and Mini buses. The latter ply around the city and levy a flat fare of 50 cents. Buses at the following bus stops will help you to get to popular destinations.

Kelang Bus Station
To Petaling Jaya, Subang Airport, Shah Alam, Port Kelang.

Bangkok Bank Bus Stand
To Selayang Baru, Segambut Dalam, Batu Caves.

Pudu Raya Bus Station
To Seri Kembangan, Sungei Besi Camp, Taman Seri Serdang, Kajang.

Mara Building Bus Stand
Buses to other states.

Taxi Services in Petaling Jaya

ComFort Corpn. – Subang Jaya
Tel 7330507

Section 14 P.J.
Tel 7565167

Syarikat Jaya – Subang Jaya
Tel 7335414

SS2 Petaling Jaya
Tel 7768272

Syarikat Kenderaan Perkasa – P.J.
Tel 7763458

Subang International
Airport
Tel 7465705

11

LIST OF EMBASSIES

Countries	Telephone	Countries	Telephone
Argentina	03-2550176	Kuwait	03-9846033
Australia	03-2423122	Libya	03-2411035
Austria	03-2484277	Netherlands	03-2431143
Bangladesh	03-2423271	New Zealand	03-2486422
Belgium	03-2485733	North Korea	03-9847110
Bolivia	03-2425146	Norway	03-2430144
Brazil	03-2548020	Pakistan	03-2418877
Brunei Darussalam	03-4562635	Philippines	03-2484233
Burma	03-2424085	Poland	03-4560940
Canada	03-2612000	Romania	03-2482065
China	03-2428495	Saudia Arabia	03-4579433
Czechoslovakia	03-2427185	Singapore	03-2616277
Denmark	03-2416088	South Korea	03-9842177
Egypt	03-4568184	Spain	03-2484868
Federal Republic of Germany	03-2429666	Sri Lanka	03-2423154
Finland	03-2611088	Sultanate of Oman	03-4575011
France	03-2484122	Sweden	03-2485981
German Democratic Republic	03-4562894	Switzerland	03-2480622
Iceland	03-7573745	Thailand	03-2488222
India	03-2617000	Turkey	03-4572225
Indonesia	03-9842011	United Kingdom	03-2541533
Iran	03-2433575		
Iraq	03-2480555	U.S.S.R.	03-4567252
Ireland	03-2985111	USA	03-2489011
Italy	03-4565122	Vietnam	03-2484036
Japan	03-2438044	Yugoslavia	03-2464561

12

LIST OF AIRLINES

Aeroflot Soviet	03-2613231
Air India	03-2420166
Air Lanka Ltd.	03-2740211
Alitalia	03-2380366
America West Airlines	03-2387057
British Airways	03-2426177
Cathay Pacific Airways Ltd.	03-2383377
China Airlines Ltd.	03-2427344
Chechoslovak Airlines	03-2380176
Delta Air Lines Inc.	03-2324700
Garuda Indonesian Airways	03-2420481
Japan Air Lines Co. Ltd.	03-2611722
K.L.M-Royal Dutch Airlines	03-2427011
Korean Airline Co. Ltd.	03-2428311
Lufthansa German Airlines	03-2614666
MAS-Malaysia Airlines	03-7463000
Northwest Orient Airlines	03-2384355
Pelangi Air Sdn. Bhd.	03-7464555
Philippine Airlines	03-2429040
Qantas Airways Ltd.	03-2389133
Royal Brunei Airlines Sdn. Bhd.	03-2426550
Royal Jordanian	03-2487500
SAS Scandinavian Airlines System	03-2426044
Sabena Belgian World Airlines	03-2425244
Saudi Arabian Airlines	03-2984150
Singapore Airlines Ltd.	03-2923122
Trans-World Airlines Inc.	03-2425466
Turkish Airlines	03-2614055
UTA French Airlines	03-2326952
United Airlines	03-2611433
Yugoslav Airlines	03-2419245

LIST OF RESTAURANTS

Chinese Food	Telephone
Restaurant Sze Chuan (KL) Sdn. Bhd. 42-3, Jalan Sultan Ismail	03-2482806

Indian Food

Bangles Restaurant Sdn. Bhd. 60A, Jalan Tuanku Abdul Rahman	03-2983780
Bilal Restoran (Indian) 33, Jalan Ampang	03-2380804
Devi Annapoorna Restaurant 94, Lorong Maarof	03-2556443
Lakshmi Vilas Restaurant 57, Leboh Ampang	03-2383523
Omar Khayam Restaurant 5, Jalan Medan Tuanku	03-2911016
Shiraz Restaurant Medan Tuanku	03-2922625
Tandoor Restaurant Sdn. Bhd. 21, Jalan Maharajalela	03-2433773

Japanese Food

Edogin Japanese Restaurant Com. Sdn. Bhd. 207-A, Jalan Tun Razak	03-2610522

Korean Food

Koryo-Won Korean Restaurant Sdn. Bhd. Komplek Antarabangsa	03-2427655

Russian Food

Troika Restaurant Komplek Kewangan	03-2616734

13

Siamese Food

Sri Siam (KL) Sdn. Bhd. 14, Jalan Utara	03-9843007

Western Food

A & W of Malaysia Sdn. Bhd. 118, Jalan Tuanku Abdul Rahman	03-2983218
Coliseum Restaurant 98, Jalan Tuanku Abdul Rahman	03-2926270
Esquire Kitchen Sdn. Bhd. 24-B, Jalan Bukit Bintang	03-2485006
Kentucky Fried Chicken Co. Sdn. Bhd. 120, Jalan Tuanku Abdul Rahman	03-2921207
McDonald's Malaysia Menara Kewangan	03-2305577
Restoran The Ship 40-1, Jalan Sultan Ismail	03-2418805
Shakey's Pizza Sdn. Bhd. Bukit Bintang Plaza	03-2437339

Malay Food

Bunga Raya Restaurant Level 2, Putra World Trade Centre	03-2933888
Jamal Bersaudara Jalan Raja Abdullah, Kampong Baru	03-2923120
Nelayan Floating Restaurant Titiwangsa Lake Gardens	03-4228600
Rasa Utara Bukit Bintang Plaza, Jalan Bukit Bintang	03-2438234

14

LIST OF TRAVEL AGENCIES

Name of Co	Telephone
1 ACE Tours & Travel Sdn. Bhd.	03-2439155
2 Air Langkawi Travel & Tours Sdn. Bhd.	03-2988705
3 Airlines Holidays Sdn. Bhd.	03-2380221
4 Airport Tours and Travel Services Sdn. Bhd.	03-7033733
5 Boustead Travel Services Sdn. Bhd.	03-2417022
6 Crescent Voyage & Tours Sdn. Bhd.	03-2616004
7 Dinners World Travel (M) Sdn. Bhd.	03-2613522
8 Ganesh Travel Agencies Sdn. Bhd.	03-2938621
9 Genting Highlands Tours & Promotion Sdn. Bhd.	03-2613833
10 Harpers Travel (M) Sdn. Bhd.	03-2322200
11 Holiday Limousine & Tours Sdn. Bhd.	03-2412779
12 International Tours Sdn. Bhd.	03-2325087
13 Ken Air Services Sdn. Bhd.	03-2433722
14 Kuala Lumpur Golf Tours (M) Sdn. Bhd.	03-2432689
15 Langkawi Travel & Tours Sdn. Bhd.	03-9581762
16 Maju Mehar Singh Travel & Tours Sdn. Bhd.	03-2481451
17 Mansfield Travel Sdn. Bhd.	03-2924724
18 Mayflower Acme Tours Sdn. Bhd.	03-6267182
19 Mimaland Tours & Travel Sdn. Bhd.	03-2427192
20 Nam Ho Travel Service (M) Sdn. Bhd.	03-2480233
21 Orient Vacation Sdn. Bhd.	03-2618299
22 Sam Fo Holidays Sdn. Bhd.	03-2325825
23 Scenic Holidays Sdn. Bhd.	03-2424522
24 Siakson (M) Sdn. Bhd.	03-2484339
25 Sime Darby Travel Sdn. Bhd.	03-2922177
26 Sri America Travel Corporation Sdn. Bhd.	03-2429155
27 Tioman Express Sdn. Bhd.	03-2305266
28 Ubaidullah & Co Sdn. Bhd.	03-2920459
29 Vacation Planners Sdn. Bhd.	03-2935280
30 World Link Travel Sdn. Bhd.	03-2427888

NOTES

NOTES

NOTES